Discipline of World

Bedatri Anand

Sharda Kumari

Utakars Anand

Kanhaiya Jee Anand

TANEESHA PUBLISHERS

Title   :   Discipline of World

Author   :   Kanhaiya Jee Anand

Edition   :   1st (February, 2024)

ISBN   :   9788196942519

Published by

Regd. Add.: 254, Khuriyakhatta No. 10, Bindukhatta,
Lalkuan, Nainital - 262402, Uttarakhand, India
Website : www.taneeshapublishers.in
E-mail : taneeshapublishers@gmail.com
Phone : +91 845481 2712, +91 976041 7980

Printed by :
Manipal Technologies Limited, Bengaluru - 560001, Karnataka

Dedicated To Beloved
Mrs. Draupdi Devi (Mother) and
Late Rcp Singh and All Family

INDEX

Basic Understanding & Introduction

Life is a Race, a Journey, a fixed journey which starts from Birth to Death. Birth is the Starting Point and Death is the Destination. Take an Example of Journey from Patna to Delhi by Train,we can find that some Passenger moving in AC, some one in General Boggy. General is mainly full then what should be the condition of one passenger, Passenger is not sitting,while Passenger in the AC is in the comfort zone. There is a Passenger before starting the Journey and there is a Passenger after Journey. This is true, There is life before Birth and there is life after death.

The above technology is well understood by Lord Shankracharya,Lord Krishna,Lord Rama,Lord Shiva,Lord Vishnu,Lord Budha,Lord Mahavir Jain,Lord Guru Nanakdev Ji,Lord Jesus,Prophet Mohammed. and other powerful Sant and Muni in the world. There is a Science book Shiv Puran,Vishnu Puran,Surya Puran,Geeta etc which is a guideline for further Research to discover and invent further. In the above Book we studied and practically researched the Geeta.

गीता सुगीता कर्तव्या किमन्यै: शास्त्रविस्तरै: ।
या स्वयं पद्मनाभस्य मुखपद्माद्विनि: सृता

Different Community

Prarthana-

शान्ताकारं भुजगशयनं पद्मनाभं सुरेशं

विश्वाधारं गगनसदृशं मेघवर्णं शुभाङ्गम् ।

लक्ष्मीकान्तं कमलनयनं योगिभिर्ध्यानगम्यम्

वन्दे विष्णुं भवभयहरं सर्वलोकैकनाथम् ॥

Wherever there is family,there are differences,differences need to be resolved by way of Nature and GEETA is the one wonder which has a solution to every life. This is not only Epic,this is a Practical research book on nature and every individual in this world following the practicality of Geeta.

Great Saint of India and World mainly- Lord Shiva who is immortal to follow the technology of Chapter 1 to 18, Lord Shiva is itself GEETA and Still lives on Earth.

Lord Vishnu,Brahma followed the similar technology to become immortal.

Ashwatthama, King Mahabali, Vedvyasa, Hanuman, Vibhishana, Kripacharya, Parashurama and Rishi Markandeya followed the similar path and received a place to become the Immortal.

The Greatest Saint in the world who proposed a different way of life is as under.

JUDAISM & CHRISTINITY COMMUNITY- Abraham & JESUS strictly followed the practicality of GITA Chapter-3,12,13,14,15,16,17 & 18. Christinity has their own Way of Life.

Jewish believe **there's only one God who has established a covenant—or special agreement—with them**.Main theme of Judaism is that the neighbor should be Happy. Main theme of Christinity Community is Healing, Maintenance of Health and Protection. The practice of the Jesus Prayer is integrated into the Mental, Physical and Spiritual.

The Major activity in this Community to DEVELOP THE MANGAL MAITRI or POSITIVITY.

MUSLIM COMMUNITY- Paigamber MOHAMMAD followed the Chapter-12.Islam have own Way of Life. Meaning of ISLAM-"**Bismillah Allahu Akbar**" or SURRENDER TO GOD. This Community does not teach any Meditation except Pray in Surrender Pose. Community reciting the Quran.Gents should be devotee of Women as women is the NATURE/GOD hence safety and Control is essential for the Women.

BUDDHISM COMMUNITY-**Lord** Budha followed the Geeta and practiced the Chapter-3,6,7,8,12,13,14,15,16,17 & 18 and as per social condition he himself taught the practical view of above Chapters for 45 year and he changed the social condition of World.His Chanting Mantra is-

Buddham Saranam Gacchami, Dhammam Saranam Gachhami, Shangham Saranam Gachhami.

To become healthy (To control of Lust,anger and Greed) and free from material attachment in all respect,Main Teaching is of strictly follow the Ayurvedic lifestyle,Perform Panch sheel/Eight Sheel,

Anapana Meditation,Vipassana Technology and Practice the Mangal Maitri to enrich the Yagya (Sacrifice), Dana (Charity) and Tapasya (austerities or penances)

JAINISM COMMUNITY Strictly practicing the Chapter-3,6,7,8,12,13.14.15.16.17 & 18, JAIN also has its own Strict Way of Life.Much focussing on Chapter no-18.

His Chanting mantra is Jai Jinendra and **NAVKAR MANTRA IS-**

Ṇamō Arihantāṇaṁ,Ṇamō Siddhāṇaṁ,Ṇamō Ayariyāṇaṁ,Ṇamō Uvajjhāyāṇaṁ,Ṇamō Lōē Savva Sāhūṇaṁ,Ēsōpañcaṇamōkkārō, savvapāvappaṇāsaṇō,Maṅgalā ṇaṁ ca savvēsiṁ, paḍamama havaī maṅgalaṁ.

Main teaching is to follow the Ayurvedic lifestyle, Non-violence, Ahimsa, Aparigraha and Moksha is achieved to follow Astangik marg,perform Sāmāyika Meditation which is done for 48 mins in peace and silence.

SIKHISM COMMUNITY Strictly followed the Chapter-3,6,12,13.14,15,16,17 & 18. KHALSA have their own strict Way of Life.

Mantra is-**Waheguru ii ka Khalsa, sri Waheguru ji ki fateh.**

There are three core tenets of the Sikh religion: Meditation upon and devotion to the Creator, truthful living, and service to humanity.

Naam Japna that is meditation on God through reciting, chanting, singing and concentration on Him

ZOROASTRIAN COMMUNITY follow Chapter-3, 12, 13, 14, 15, 16, 17 & 18 and have their own Way of Life. **Mantra-Ashem** Vohu (**"Truth is best (of all that is) good. As desired, as desired, truth.**)

The practice of Zoroastrianism is **"Good thoughts, good words, good deeds"**

AJIVIKA COMMUNITY-Followed the Chapter-3, 4, 5, 12, 13, 14, 15, 16, & 17 and have their own way of Life. Makhali Ghoshal is the founder of Ajivika Movement. Main Idea is that whatever is happening in the world is NIYTI (Law of Nature). Humans have to Work without attachment,Lust and Greed.

SANATAN (HINDUISM) COMMUNITY have the option to follow all chapters from 1 to 18 from Birth to Death in different different stages.Sanatan people follow the 16 Sanskar,which comes in different phases of life which includes the 18 chapter of GITA. There are Nine works divided which indicate to perform any work with devotion,that work will give peace to the concerned People. Similarly all Saints or GOD follow the different chapter of Geeta itself and have Own Way of Life.

Like Gandhi ji tried to follow the Chapter-3,6,8,12,13,14,15,16,17 & 18 but failed as he was unable to detach from English Ruler and their benefit.Result Partition of Country and there was death of Million people.

Science of Gita

IMPORTANT SLOKA OF GITA-

यदा यदा ही धर्मस्य ग्लानिर्भवति भारत ।

अभ्युत्थानमधर्मस्य तदात्मानम सृज्याहम ॥

परित्राणाय साधूनां विनाशाय च दुष्कृताम ।

धर्म संस्थापनार्थाय संभवामि युगे युगे ॥

जन्म कर्म च मे दिव्यमेवं यो वेत्ति तत्त्वतः ।

त्यक्त्वा देहं पुनर्जन्म नैति मामेति सोऽर्जुन ॥

वीतरागभयक्रोधा मन्मया मामुपाश्रिताः ।

बहवो ज्ञानतपसा पूता मद्भावमागताः ॥

ये यथा मां प्रपद्यन्ते तांस्तथैव भजाम्यहम्

मम वर्त्मानुवर्तन्ते मनुष्याः पार्थ सर्वशः ॥

काङ्क्षन्तः कर्मणां सिद्धिं यजन्त इह देवताः ।

क्षिप्रं हि मानुषे लोके सिद्धिर्भवति कर्मजा ॥

चातुर्वर्ण्यं मया सृष्टं गुणकर्मविभागशः ।

तस्य कर्तारमपि मां विद्ध्यकर्तारमव्ययम् ॥
न मां कर्माणि लिम्पन्ति न मे कर्मफले स्पृहा ।
इति मां योऽभिजानाति कर्मभिर्न स बध्यते ॥
एवं ज्ञात्वा कृतं कर्म पूर्वैरपि मुमुक्षुभिः ।
कुरु कर्मैव तस्माच्त्वं पूर्वैः पूर्वतरं कृतम् ॥

Chapter-1 Arjun Bishad Yog- This describes the family position,Where there is family there is GITA.Family may be of human only,Human and animal etc etc.There is two part of this Chapter Ist part-Duryodhna was happy to see their Warrier.in same time Pandava is aggressive in which Arjuna reached in between both warrier and he feels bishad to think about family .Lord Krishna got opportunity to talk on GITA.

Chapter-2 Sankhya Yog-There must be analytical knowledge of the family or social condition.and decision required as per situation and without lust and Greed.

Analytical Thinking is the route of Sankhya Yog.

Chapter-3 Karm Yog-Karm is the theme of all results,hence Karma is always superior to Gyan. To run the family there is need of Karm,Karm must be without attachment of Lust,anger and Greed.

SACRIFICE (YAJNAS) is the route to improve our Karma.

Chapter-4 Jnana Karma Sanyasa Yoga-In this chapter Lord Krishna teaches to regulate the **LIFE ENERGY** by performing Yog of Pranayam to control the Inner kumbhaka and External Kumbhaka.

Chapter-5 Karma Sanyas Yog-Krishna teaches a method to control the **Sense,Mind & Intellect** by controlling the length of incoming breadth and outgoing breadth and control of Mind at Third Eye.

Chapter-6 Self Control Yog-Krishna teaches a method to perform Dhyan(watching the Inhalation and exhalation to bring mind at door of

Nose and watching externally and internally without action on any happening to free from material contamination.

Control of the whole Human body is the key requirement.

Chapter-7 Krisna Described the Gyan Vigyan Yog-

Yog through the Realization of Divine Knowledge.Krishna further teaches the technology to control the Earth, water, fire, air, space, mind, intellect, and ego—these are eight components of material energy.

Understanding of Material Energy is the real requirement.

My divine *Yogmaya* **energy** is Prakriti and Purusha.

Prakriti is yogamaya.Kali,or Shakti is yogamaya. It is the combination of Sattva, Rajas and Tamas.

Chapter-8 Krishna teaches the Akshara Brahma Yoga-The Yog of the Eternal God.Krishna described the method to attain the permanent peace in life to bring mind and respiration to Anahat Chakra,close the all gate,bring mind and respiration to Third Eye position and again fully close the all door gate and bring mind and respiration at top of head,this will separate the mind and respiration from body and will bring life to PEACE.This needs a practice.

There are three gates leading to the hell of self-destruction for the soul—lust, anger, and greed. Therefore, one should abandon all three.

Krishna teaches human body is the product of Akash, vayu, Agni, Water, Earth, Man, Budhi and Ahankar **PERMANENT PEACE** is the key requirement of every creature.

Chapter 9: Krishna teaches Raja Vidya Yog-Yog through the King of Sciences, he describes the Universe as in Nature/Krishna.

Krishna has Natural Power and itself a Universe.

Chapter 10:Vibhūti Yog-Yog through Appreciating the Infinite Opulences of God.

Krishna is available in different forms in nature like the Peepal tree is krishna.

The Living Element which has the quality of Krishna is available on Earth.

Different Form is the real requirement.

Chapter 11: Krishna explored the Vishwarūp Darśhan Yog-
Yog through Beholding the Cosmic Form of God.

Vishwarup Darshan is the key of this YOG

Chapter 12: Krishna described the Bhakti Yoga-The Yog of Devotion

Two methods of Devotion are I. Personal form and II. Formless Brahman.

While formless has to define.This is achieved after long practice.

Krishna described Gyan is better than Practice,karm is better than Gyan and Dhyan is better than the Work and sacrifice is far better than the Dhyan.

When Atma performing yag in Atma it gives peace,which is far better than all other Work(Karm)

Sacrifice is the key to achieve the realization fast.

Devotion is human nature,but it should be strengthened to deeply devote to GOD.

Chapter 13: Krishna discussed Kṣhetra Kṣhetrajña Vibhāg Yog-Yog through Distinguishing the Field and the Knower of the Field.

What are *prakriti* and *puruṣh*, and what are *kṣhetra* and *kṣhetrajña*?

This body is termed as *kṣhetra* (the field of activities), and the one who knows this body is called *kṣhetrajña* (the knower of the field)

When the *puruṣh* (individual soul) seated in *prakriti* (the material nature or energy) desires to enjoy the three *guṇas*, attachment to them becomes the cause of its birth in superior and inferior wombs.

Chapter 14: Guṇa Traya Vibhāg Yog-Yog through Understanding the Three Modes of Material Nature

Prakṛiti, is the womb.

The material energy consists of three *guṇas* (modes)—*sattva* (goodness), *rajas* (passion), and *tamas* (ignorance). These modes bind the eternal soul to the perishable body.

Sattva binds one to material happiness; *rajas* conditions the soul toward actions; and *tamas* clouds wisdom and binds one to delusion.

Sometimes goodness (*sattva*) prevails over passion (*rajas*) and ignorance (*tamas*). Sometimes passion (*rajas*) dominates goodness (*sattva*) and ignorance (*tamas)*, and at other times ignorance (*tamas*) overcomes goodness (*sattva*) and passion (*rajas*).

Those who die with predominance of *sattva* reach the pure abodes (which are free from *rajas* and *tamas*) of the learned. Those who die with prevalence of the mode of passion are born among people driven by work, while those dying in the mode of ignorance take birth in the animal kingdom.

Chapter 15: Puruṣhottam Yoga-The Yog of the Supreme Divine Personality.

They speak of an eternal *aśhvatth* tree with its roots above and branches below. Its leaves are the Vedic hymns, and one who knows the secret of this tree is the knower of the Vedas.

It is I who take the form of the fire of digestion in the stomachs of all living beings, and combine with the incoming and outgoing breaths, to digest and assimilate the four kinds of foods.

Chapter 16: Krishna Described the Daivāsura Sampad Vibhāg Yog-Yog through Discerning the Divine and Demoniac Natures.

Demoniac-The qualities of those who possess a demoniac nature are hypocrisy, arrogance, conceit, anger, harshness, and ignorance.They possess neither purity, nor good conduct, nor even truthfulness.

Divine Nature-The divine qualities lead to liberation, while the demoniac qualities are the cause for a continuing destiny of bondage. Grieve.As you were born with saintly virtues.

There are three gates leading to the hell of self-destruction for the soul—lust, anger, and greed. Therefore, one should abandon all three.

Chapter 17:Śhraddhā Traya Vibhāg Yog-Yog through Discerning the Three Divisions of Faith.

The Supreme Divine Personality said: Every human being is born with innate faith, which can be of three kinds—*sāttvic, rājasic,* or *tāmasic.*

He also described the type of People and their feeding habits.

"Om Tat Sat" If faith in GOD talked Om Tat Sat.

Whatever acts of sacrifice, charity, or penance are done without faith, are termed as *"Asat.*

Chapter 18-Krishna described the Mokṣha Sanyās Yog-Yog through the Perfection of Renunciation and Surrender.

Sacrifice,Charity and Penance is the route of Moksha sanyas Yog.

Krishna also described the 4 types of people Brahmin,Kshatriya,Vaishya and Shudra based on their quality or Guna.

HENCE

- Why do we worry unnecessarily? Why do we fear in vain? Who can kill ourself? The soul is neither born nor does it die.

- Whatever happened, was for the best. Whatever is happening, is for the best. Do not repent the past. Do not worry about the future. The present goes on.

- What have we lost, that we cry? What did we bring with we that we lost? What did we create that got destroyed? We did not bring anything with you; whatever we had was taken from here.

Whatever we took, was taken from Him (God). We came empty-handed, We will go empty-handed. Today what is ours was someone else's yesterday and will be yet someone else's tomorrow. We are happy thinking it is ours. It is this happiness that is the cause of our sorrow.

- Change is the law of Nature. What we perceive as death, is actually life. One moment we have millions, the next we are poor. Mine-yours, big-small, relations-strangers; remove these ideas from your thoughts, remove them from your mind, then all will be ours and we will be for all.

- Our body does not belong to us, nor do we belong to the body. It is the mode of fire, water, air, earth and the sky and will return to these. However, the soul is immortal, Then what are we? Dedicate yourself to God. He is the best guide. He who knows his power is eternally free from fear, worry or grief.

- Whatever we do, dedicate it to God. Only through this will we experience eternal bliss.

Jews and Christianity

JUDAISM & CHRISTINITY- Abraham & JESUS strictly followed the practicality of GITA Chapter-3,12,13,14,15,16,17 & 18.

Christinity has their own Way of Life.

Jewish believe **there's only one God who has established a covenant—or special agreement—with them**.Main theme of Judaism is that the neighbor should be Happy. Main theme of Christian Community is Healing, Maintenance of Health and Protection.

The practice of the Jesus Prayer is integrated into the Mental, Physical and Spiritual

The main Practice of Christianity is to Develop the Mangal Maitri.

JUDAISM-

The Hebrew Bible or Tanakh is the main religious text of the **JEWS**.

It has been composed in different countries by different authors in the time period from 600 to 100 BC. Basically the Hebrew Bible is a compilation of three different scriptures. which are the basis of ancient Jewish tradition. So there are three parts of the tanakh-

Taurat:- It consists of five books. Which was composed by Moses. These five books are the foundation of the Jewish tradition.

Navim:- It contains the books of the Prophet or prophets, whose number is eight.

Ketavim:- It contains eleven compositions of worship and prophecies of God. A large part of Hazrat Dawood's Zaboor (Tehillim) is found in this part.

The first part of the Christian scripture Bible is a version of the Old Testament. Judaism is **the world's oldest monotheistic Community,** dating back nearly 4,000 years. Followers of Judaism believe in one God who revealed himself through ancient prophets. The history of Judaism is essential to understanding the Jewish faith, which has a rich heritage of law, culture and tradition.

A summary of what Jews believe about God

- God exists.
- There is only one God.
- There are no other gods.
- God can't be subdivided into different persons (unlike the Christian view of God)
- Jews should worship only one God.
- God is Transcendent: ...
- God doesn't have a body. ...
- God created the universe without help

Laws of ritual purity

The Tanakh describes circumstances in which a person who is *tahor* or ritually pure may become *tamei* or ritually impure. Some of these circumstances are contact with human corpses or graves, seminal flux, vaginal flux, menstruation, and contact with people who have become impure from any of these.In Rabbinic Judaism, Kohanim, members of the hereditary caste that served as priests in the time of the Temple, are mostly restricted from entering grave sites and touching dead bodies.During the Temple period, such priests (Kohanim) were required to eat their bread offering (Terumah) in a state of ritual purity, which laws eventually led to more rigid laws being enacted, such as hand-washing which became a requisite of all Jews before consuming ordinary bread.

Family purity

An important subcategory of the ritual purity laws relates to the segregation of menstruating women.

These laws are also known as *niddah*, literally "separation", or family purity. Vital aspects of *halakha* for traditionally observant Jews, they are not usually followed by Jews in liberal denominations.

Especially in Orthodox Judaism, the Biblical laws are augmented by Rabbinical injunctions. For example, the Torah mandates that a woman in her normal menstrual period must abstain from sexual intercourse for seven days. A woman whose menstruation is prolonged must continue to abstain for seven more days after bleeding has stopped.The Rabbis conflated ordinary *niddah* with this extended menstrual period, known in the Torah as *zavah*, and mandated that a woman may not have sexual intercourse with her husband from the time she begins her menstrual flow until seven days after it ends.

In addition, Rabbinical law forbids the husband from touching or sharing a bed with his wife during this period. Afterwards, purification can occur in a ritual bath called a mikveh

Traditional Ethiopian Jews keep menstruating women in separate huts and, similar to Karaite practice, do not allow menstruating women into their temples because of a temple's special sanctity.

Emigration to Israel and the influence of other Jewish denominations have led to Ethiopian Jews adopting more normative Jewish practices.

Life-cycle events

Life-cycle events, or rites of passage, occur throughout a Jew's life that serve to strengthen Jewish identity and bind him/her to the entire community.

- Brit milah – Welcoming male babies into the covenant through the rite of circumcision on their eighth day of life. The baby boy is also given his Hebrew name in the ceremony. A naming ceremony intended as a parallel ritual for girls, named *zeved habat* or brit bat, enjoys limited popularity.

- Bar mitzvah and Bat mitzvah – This passage from childhood to adulthood takes place when a female Jew is twelve and a male Jew is thirteen years old among Orthodox and some Conservative congregations.

- In the Reform movement, both girls and boys have their bat/bar mitzvah at age thirteen.

- This is often commemorated by having the new adults, male only in the Orthodox tradition, lead the congregation in prayer and publicly read a "portion" of the Torah.

- Marriage – Marriage is an extremely important lifecycle event. A wedding takes place under a *chuppah*, or wedding canopy, which symbolizes a happy house.

- At the end of the ceremony, the groom breaks a glass with his foot, symbolizing the continuous mourning for the destruction of the Temple, and the scattering of the Jewish people.

- Death and Mourning – Judaism has a multi-staged mourning practice. The first stage is called the shiva (literally "seven", observed for one week) during which it is traditional to sit at home and be comforted by friends and family, the second is the *shloshim* (observed for one month) and for those who have lost one of their parents, there is a third stage, *avelut yud bet chodesh*, which is observed for eleven months.

The role of the priesthood in Judaism has significantly diminished since the destruction of the Second Temple in 70 CE when priests attended to the Temple and sacrifices. The priesthood is an inherited position, and although priests no longer have any but ceremonial duties, they are still honored in many Jewish communities. Many Orthodox Jewish communities believe that they will be needed again for a future Third Temple and need to remain in readiness for future duty.

- Kohen (priest) – patrilineal descendant of Aaron, brother of Moses. In the Temple, the *kohanim* were charged with performing the sacrifices. Today, a Kohen is the first one called up at the reading of the Torah, performs the Priestly Blessing, as well as complying with other unique laws and ceremonies, including the ceremony of redemption of the first-born.

- Levi (Levite) – Patrilineal descendant of Levi the son of Jacob. In the Temple in Jerusalem, the Levites sang Psalms, performed construction, maintenance, janitorial, and guard duties, assisted the priests, and sometimes interpreted the law and Temple ritual to the public. Today, a Levite is called up second to the reading of the Torah.

BASICS OF CHRISTIANITY-

The Hebrew Bible or Tanakh is the main religious text of the **JEWS**.

It has been composed in different countries by different authors in the time period from 600 to 100 BC. Basically the Hebrew Bible is a compilation of three different scriptures. which are the basis of ancient Jewish tradition. So there are three parts of the tanakh-

Taurat:- It consists of five books. Which was composed by Moses. These five books are the foundation of the Jewish tradition.

Navim:- It contains the books of the Prophet or prophets, whose number is eight.

Ketavim:- It contains eleven compositions of worship and prophecies of God. A large part of Hazrat Dawood's Zaboor (Tehillim) is found in this part. The first part of the Christian scripture Bible is a version of the Old Testament.

Christian Community-

Christian (Christian) religion is an Abrahamic religion derived from ancient Jewish tradition. There are mainly three sects among Christians, Catholic, Protestant and Orthodox, and their religious text is the Bible. The religious site of Christians is called a cathedral. Like other Abrahamic religions, it is also a Trinity. According to Christian tradition, it started in Palestine in the first century AD, whose followers are called 'Christians'.

What are the 5 basic beliefs of Christianity?

1) Uniqueness of Jesus (Virgin Birth)-

Jesus Christ was unique in that he alone, of all who ever lived, was both God and man. The New Testament teaches the fully unified deity and humanity of **Christ**.

2) One God (The Trinity)-

Trinity, in Christian doctrine, the unity of Father, Son, and Holy Spirit as three persons in **one** Godhead.

3) Necessity of the Cross (Salvation)-

For Christians, the cross is a symbol of salvation. **It is by Christ's death on the cross that God is justified in forgiving sinners**; which he does for every sinner who acknowledges their need of salvation.

4) Resurrection and Second Coming are combined-

The **Second Coming** is a Christian and Islamic belief that Jesus will return again, after his ascension to heaven about two thousand years ago.

5) Inspiration of Scripture-

All Scripture was given by inspiration of God" (KJV and NKJV). Many of the revised or newer translations that have come about over the last century were closer to the original Greek text, but still retain the word "inspired." For example, "All Scripture is inspired by God" (NRSV, NASB, HCSB, and several others)

JESUS

The central tenet of Christianity is the belief in Jesus as the Son of God and the Messiah (Christ). Christians believe that Jesus, as the Messiah, was anointed by God as savior of humanity and hold that Jesus' coming was the fulfillment of messianic prophecies of the Old Testament. The Christian concept of messiah differs significantly from the contemporary Jewish concept.

As per Internet knowledge JESUS spent 12 years in India under Jagat Guru Shankaracharya and he studied GITA.He was also Bhakt of Lord Budha.

The core Christian belief is that through belief in and acceptance of the death and resurrection of Jesus, sinful humans can be reconciled to God, and thereby are offered salvation and the promise of eternal life.

While there have been many theological disputes over the nature of Jesus over the earliest centuries of Christian history, generally, Christians believe that Jesus is God incarnate and "true God and true man" (or both fully divine and fully human). Jesus, having become fully human, suffered the pains and temptations of a mortal man, but did not sin.

As fully God, he rose to life again. According to the New Testament, he rose from the dead,ascended to heaven, is seated at the right hand of the Father,and will ultimately return to fulfill the rest of the Messianic prophecy, including the resurrection of the dead, the Last Judgment, and the final establishment of the Kingdom of God. According to the canonical gospels of Matthew and Luke, Jesus was conceived by the Holy Spirit and born from the Virgin Mary. Little of Jesus' childhood is recorded in the canonical gospels, although infancy gospels were popular in antiquity.

In comparison, his adulthood, especially the week before his death, is well documented in the gospels contained within the New Testament, because that part of his life is believed to be most important.

The central and deepest doctrine of the Trinity Christianity is related to the inner form of God called the Trinity.

The Trinity means that there are three persons in one God - the Father, the Son and the Holy Spirit (Father, Son and Holy Ghost).

These three are equally beginningless, infinite and omnipotent because human intelligence can reach the existence of an omnipotent creator God only by the power of reason.

In fact, the doctrine of the Trinity is believed to have been taught by Jesus. The first half of the Bible shows that Judaism had a special emphasis on monotheism.

In the latter part of the Bible, Jesus still maintains that one God, teaching that I and God the Father are one (in fact the Jews executed Jesus for this reason).

Apart from this, he tells his disciples that I will send the Holy Spirit to be with you in an unmanifested form. He also considers that holy soul to be integrated with the divine qualities. Thus Jesus clearly stated that the Father, the Son and the Holy Spirit exist in one God. Later this attribute of the Triune God is given the name of Tritva. Christian theologians have tried to explain this doctrine of the Trinity with the help of the definitions of Greek and Latin philosophy in this way - three persons (Parsons) exist in the same divine nature (Nature).

The three are essentially (substantively) one. Therefore, all three have the same will power and the same intellect.

Yet there is a mutual difference between the Father, the Son, and the Holy Spirit. Father is not born from anyone.

The son assumes the perfect godhood from the father since time immemorial. This generation of a son is called generation. The creation of the Holy Spirit is called generation. The origin of the Holy Spirit is believed to be from both the father and the son and is called the procession.

The mutual difference of the three persons arises from the procreation of the Son and the transmission of the Holy Spirit, but in essence all three are one and are equally integrated with all the divine qualities. (In the Oriental Church the Holy Spirit is believed to have descended from the Father).

This doctrine has been contemplated for centuries, and many of the metaphysical notions have been falsified. Tritheism, which assumes three distinct divine elements, is clearly misleading, as it thus accepts the existence of three independent gods. According to Modalism, the Father, the Son and the Holy Spirit are three aspects of the same God that are created by creation – the Father is the Creator, the Son saves us and the Holy Spirit sanctifies us. The Church rejected this claim in the 3rd and 4th centuries, stating that there were three persons in God before the creation.

The Synod of Nissia (325 AD) has refuted all the interpretations of the Trinity according to which the Son or the Holy Spirit is considered secondary to the Father.

It is clearly declared in that assembly that father and son are essentially one. "the Father is God, the Son is God, and the Holy Spirit is God, and yet there are not three Gods but one God".

They are distinct from another: the Father has no source, the Son is begotten of the Father, and the Spirit proceeds from the Father.

Though distinct, the three persons cannot be divided from one another in being or in operation. The books of the Bible accepted by the Orthodox, Catholic, and Protestant churches vary somewhat, with Jews accepting only the Hebrew Bible as canonical; however, there is substantial overlap.

These variations are a reflection of the range of traditions, and of the councils that have convened on the subject. Every version of the Old Testament always includes the books of the Tanakh, the canon of the Hebrew Bible.

The Catholic and Orthodox canons, in addition to the Tanakh, also include the <u>deuterocanonical books</u> as part of the Old Testament.

These books appear in the Septuagint, but are regarded by Protestants to be apocryphal. However, they are considered to be important historical documents which help to inform the understanding of words, grammar, and syntax used in the historical period of their conception.

Some versions of the Bible include a separate Apocrypha section between the Old Testament and the New Testament.

The New Testament, originally written in Koine Greek, contains 27 books which are agreed upon by all major churches.

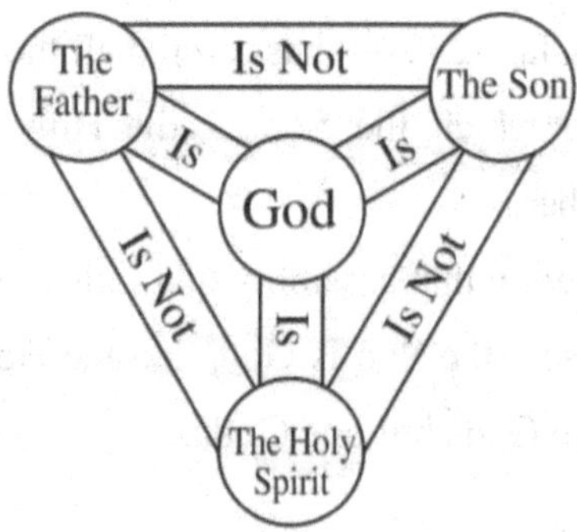

The 7 Basics of Christianity: God. You need to understand that God consists of three equal persons: ...

- Jesus. You need to have a big picture understanding to know His importance. ...
- The Holy Spirit. The Holy Spirit is God's presence on earth. ...
- The Bible. The Bible is God's Word. ...
- Prayer. ...
- Grace. ...
- Community

Catholic-

In Catholicism, the Pope is considered the supreme religious leader.

Orthodox-

The Orthodox do not believe in the Pope of Rome, but believe in the Patriarch of their respective national confederacy and are traditionalists.

Protestant-

Protestants do not believe in any pope and instead have full faith in the Holy Bible. Imitation was forbidden in the Middle Ages for the public to read the Bible. Due to which people did not have proper knowledge of Christianity. Some bishops and clergy did not understand it in accordance with true Christian religion and began to interpret the Bible in their own languages, which was opposed by the Pope. Those bishops and clergy separated from the Pope and established a new denomination called Protestant.

CATHOLICS

Catholics believe that their religious organization continues the tradition of the early Christian organization and is its sole heir. They believe that the bread and wine that is consumed in their prayer rituals become the mass and blood in a religious sense that is consumed by the praying person.

This was not the case in Protestant customs. Catholics consider the Pope to be the supreme head of Christianity on earth, which Protestants do not believe. In this religious organization, there is a priest of a higher rank above each priest and finally the Pope is above all.

In Catholicism, priests are not allowed to marry and have to practice celibacy for life.Some women also give their lives in the name of religion and remain virgins for life. These are called "nuns". When she takes the oath to become a nun, she is "married to Jesus" wearing wedding robes in a formal ceremony. These nuns are often teachers in schools run by Catholic organizations.

Catholic Missionary have three work is as under-

1. Construction of Church and a way of establishing for Celibacy for life,teaching Bible to create Father.Father is who is establishing for Celibacy for life,Serving to Society.

2. Establishing a School to teach the Children and Establishing the Hospital to serve the Society.

3. Teaching to Women to create Sister,Sister she is getting knowledge to serve the Human.Some sister married to Jesus and becoming NUN and lives in the name of religion and remain virgins for life.

Protestantism

Pentecostalism is a form of Christianity that emphasizes the work of the Holy Spirit and the direct experience of the presence of God by the believer. Pentecostals believe that faith must be powerfully experiential, and not something found merely through ritual or thinking. Pentecostalism is energetic and dynamic. It emerged as a result of the Protestant reformist movement in the sixteenth century. This religion is strongly opposed to Roman Catholicism. Its main belief is that the scriptures (Bible) are the real source of revealed truth and not traditions etc.

It is often heard about Protestants that they are divided into innumerable denominations, but in fact 94 percent of all Protestants are included in only five denominations, namely: Lutheran, Calvinist, Anglican, Baptist and Methodist.

Pentecostal

Several sects called Pentecostals originated in the 20th century.

Altogether their membership is said to be around one crore.

Those sects are named after the festival of Pentecost.

Sentimentality and the importance of the gifts of the Holy Spirit are the main characteristics of those sects.

Christian Science

Mary Baker Eddy (1821–1911 AD) saw Jesus as a spiritual healer. His main principle is that sin and disease are the illusions of our senses, which can be removed by Mind Cure. He founded a sect called Christian Science, which is still very influential in America today.

Do We Love Our Neighbor Better.They Helped Every One His Neighbor, And Every One Said To His Brother, Be Of Good Courage.

Christian Science Nurses- Christian Science nurses are first and foremost dedicated Christian Scientists. They are trained to provide practical care that meets the patient's physical needs and is consistent with the theology of Christian Science. The heart of their work is to minister to a patient's spiritual need for love, comfort, and healing. The nurse should be cheerful, orderly, punctual, patient, full of faith, — receptive to Truth and Love.

Praying for World- Praying for our world can seem like more than we can take on when we're facing challenges in our own lives.

But as we open our hearts to our neighbors' needs, we in turn feel the infinite love of God that lifts us all.

ORTHODOX-

The Orthodox or Eastern Orthodox Church is one of the three major denominations of Christianity. Divided into Latin in the west, and Greek centers in the east by the 11th century, Eastern Byzantine Orthodoxy broke away from Western Catholicism and rejected papal authority in 1054 AD as a result of the Christian Empire.

Sometimes it is also called Eastern Orthodoxy.

- The Orthodox Christian faith is that faith "handed once to the saints" (Jude 3), passed on to the apostles by Jesus Christ, and then handed down from one generation to the next within the Church, without adding anything or taking anything away.

Orthodoxy is adherence to correct or accepted creeds, especially in religion. Orthodoxy within Christianity refers to acceptance of the doctrines defined by various creeds and ecumenical councils in Antiquity, but different Churches accept different creeds and councils. Such differences of opinion have developed for numerous reasons, including language and cultural barriers.

The sole purpose of Orthodox Christianity is the salvation of every human person, uniting him to Christ in the Church, transforming him in holiness, and imparting eternal life.

Salvation is defined as being saved from or delivered from sin or harm.

Islam

ISLAM- Paigamber MOHAMMAD follwed the Chapter-12.Islam have own Way of Life.

Meaning of ISLAM-**"Bismillah Allahu Akbar"**.SURRENDER TO GOD. Community does not teach any meditation except Pray in Surrender Pose.. Each Muslim has to Recite the Quran.Normally Males become the Devotee of Women as women is the NATURE/GOD and Controlling the Women with help of Mollana etc.

BASICS-

A *Muslim* the word for a follower of Islam, is the active participle of the same verb form, and means "submitter (to God)" or "one who surrenders (to God)". The word "Islam" ("submission") sometimes has distinct connotations in its various occurrences in the Quran. Some verses stress the quality of Islam as an internal spiritual state: "Whoever God wills to guide, He opens their heart to Islam.

Abu al-Qasim Muhammad ibn Abdullah ibn Abd al-Muttalib ibn Hashim was born in Mecca about the year 570 and his birthday is believed to be in the month of Rabi' al-awwal. He belonged to the Banu Hashim clan, part of the Quraysh tribe, which was one of Mecca's prominent families, although it appears less prosperous during Muhammad's early lifetime. Tradition places the year of Muhammad's birth as corresponding with the Year of the Elephant, which is named after the failed destruction of Mecca that year by the Abraha, Yemen's king, who supplemented his army with elephants.Alternatively some 20th century scholars have suggested different years, such as 568 or 569.

Muhammad's father, Abdullah, died almost six months before he was born. According to Islamic tradition, soon after birth he was sent to live with a Bedouin family in the desert, as desert life was considered healthier for infants; some western scholars reject this tradition's historicity.

Muhammad stayed with his foster-mother, Halimah bint Abi Dhuayb, and her husband until he was two years old. At the age of six, Muhammad lost his biological mother Amina to illness and became an orphan. For the next two years, until he was eight years old, Muhammad was under the guardianship of his paternal grandfather Abd al-Muttalib, of the Banu Hashim clan until his death.

He then came under the care of his uncle Abu Talib, the new leader of the Banu Hashim. According to Islamic historian William Montgomery Watt there was a general disregard by guardians in taking care of weaker members of the tribes in Mecca during the 6th century, "Muhammad's guardians saw that he did not starve to death, but it was hard for them to do more for him, especially as the fortunes of the clan of Hashim seem to have been declining at that time."

In his teens, Muhammad accompanied his uncle on Syrian trading journeys to gain experience in commercial trade.

Islamic tradition states that when Muhammad was either nine or twelve while accompanying the Meccans' caravan to Syria, he met a Christian monk or hermit named Bahira who is said to have foreseen Muhammad's career as a prophet of God. Little is known of Muhammad during his later youth as available information is fragmented, making it difficult to separate history from legend.

It is known that he became a merchant and "was involved in trade between the Indian Ocean and the Mediterranean Sea." Due to his upright character he acquired the nickname "al-Amin" (Arabic: الامين), meaning "faithful, trustworthy" and "al-Sadiq" meaning "truthful" and was sought out as an impartial arbitrator.His reputation attracted a proposal in 595 from Khadijah, a successful businesswoman. Muhammad consented to the marriage, which by all accounts was a happy one.

Several years later, according to a narration collected by historian Ibn Ishaq, Muhammad was involved with a well-known story about setting the Black Stone in place in the wall of the Kaaba in 605 CE.

The Black Stone, a sacred object, was removed during renovations to the Kaaba.

The Meccan leaders could not agree which clan should return the Black Stone to its place.

They decided to ask the next man who comes through the gate to make that decision; that man was the 35-year-old Muhammad.

This event happened five years before the first revelation by Gabriel to him. He asked for a cloth and laid the Black Stone in its center. The clan leaders held the corners of the cloth and together carried the Black Stone to the right spot, then Muhammad laid the stone, satisfying the honor of all.

Muhammad's life is traditionally defined into two periods: pre-hijra (emigration) in Mecca (from 570 to 622), and post-hijra in Medina (from 622 until 632).

Muhammad is said to have had thirteen wives in total (although two have ambiguous accounts, Rayhana bint Zayd and Maria al-Qibtiyya, as wife or concubine). Eleven of the thirteen marriages occurred after the migration to Medina. At the age of 25, Muhammad married the wealthy Khadijah bint Khuwaylid who was 40 years old. The marriage lasted for 25 years and was a happy one.

Muhammad did not enter into marriage with another woman during this marriage.After Khadijah's death, Khawla bint Hakim suggested to Muhammad that he should marry Sawda bint Zama, a Muslim widow, or Aisha, daughter of Um Ruman and Abu Bakr of Mecca. Muhammad is said to have asked for arrangements to marry both.Muhammad's marriages after the death of Khadijah were contracted mostly for political or humanitarian reasons.

The women were either widows of Muslims killed in battle and had been left without a protector, or belonged to important families or clans with whom it was necessary to honor and strengthen alliances.

According to traditional sources, Aisha was six or seven years old when betrothed to Muhammad,with the marriage not being consummated until she had reached puberty at the age of nine or ten years old.

She was therefore a virgin at marriage.Modern Muslim authors who calculate Aisha's age based on other sources of information, such as a hadith about the age difference between Aisha and her sister Asma, estimate that she was over thirteen and perhaps in her late teens at the time of her marriage.

After migration to Medina, Muhammad, who was then in his fifties, married several more women.

Muhammad performed household chores such as preparing food, sewing clothes, and repairing shoes.

He is also said to have accustomed his wives to dialogue; he listened to their advice, and the wives debated and even argued with him.

Khadijah is said to have had four daughters with Muhammad (Ruqayyah bint Muhammad, Umm Kulthum bint Muhammad, Zainab bint Muhammad, Fatimah Zahra) and two sons (Abd-Allah ibn Muhammad and Qasim ibn Muhammad, who both died in childhood).

All but one of his daughters, Fatimah, died before him. Some Shi'a scholars contend that Fatimah was Muhammad's only daughter. Maria al-Qibtiyya bore him a son named Ibrahim ibn Muhammad, but the child died when he was two years old. Nine of Muhammad's wives survived him.Aisha, who became known as Muhammad's favourite wife in Sunni tradition, survived him by decades and was instrumental in helping assemble the scattered sayings of Muhammad that form the Hadith literature for the Sunni branch of Islam.

Muhammad's descendants through Fatimah are known as *sharifs*, *syeds* or *sayyids*.

These are honorific titles in Arabic, *sharif* meaning 'noble' and *sayed* or *sayyid* meaning 'lord' or 'sir'. As Muhammad's only descendants, they are respected by both Sunni and Shi'a, though the Shi'a place much more emphasis and value on their distinction. Zayd ibn Haritha was a slave that Muhammad bought, freed, and then adopted as his son. He also had a wetnurse. According to a BBC summary, "the Prophet Muhammad did not try to abolish slavery, and bought, sold, captured, and owned slaves himself. But he insisted that slave owners treat their slaves well and stressed the virtue of freeing slaves. Muhammad treated slaves as human beings and clearly held some in the highest esteem".

Following the attestation to the oneness of God, the belief in Muhammad's prophethood is the main aspect of the Islamic faith. Every Muslim proclaims in *Shahadah*: "I testify that there is no god but God, and I testify that Muhammad is a Messenger of God."

The Shahadah is the basic creed or tenet of Islam. Islamic belief is that ideally the Shahadah is the first words a newborn will hear; children are taught it immediately and it will be recited upon death. Muslims repeat the shahadah in the call to prayer (*adhan*) and the prayer itself. Non-Muslims wishing to convert to Islam are required to recite the creed.

In Islamic belief, Muhammad is regarded as the last prophet sent by God. Quran 10:37 states that "...it (the Quran) is a confirmation of (revelations) that went before it, and a fuller explanation of the Book—wherein there is no doubt—from The Lord of the Worlds." Similarly, Quran 46:12 states "...And before this was the book of Moses, as a guide and a mercy. And this Book confirms (it)...", while 2:136 commands the believers of Islam to "Say: we believe in God and that which is revealed unto us, and that which was revealed unto Abraham and Ishmael and Isaac and Jacob and the tribes, and that which Moses and Jesus received, and which the prophets received from their Lord. We make no distinction between any of them, and unto Him we have surrendered."

Muslim tradition credits Muhammad with several miracles or supernatural events.For example, many Muslim commentators and some Western scholars have interpreted the Surah 54:1–2 as referring to Muhammad splitting the Moon in view of the Quraysh when they began persecuting his followers. Western historian of Islam Denis Gril believes the Quran does not overtly describe Muhammad performing miracles, and the supreme miracle of Muhammad is identified with the Quran itself. According to Islamic tradition, Muhammad was attacked by the people of Ta'if and was badly injured.

The tradition also describes an angel appearing to him and offering retribution against the assailants. It is said that Muhammad rejected the offer and prayed for the guidance of the people of Ta'if. The Sunnah represents actions and sayings of Muhammad (preserved in reports known as Hadith) and covers a broad array of activities and beliefs ranging from religious rituals, personal hygiene, and burial of the dead to the mystical questions involving the love between humans and God.

The Sunnah is considered a model of emulation for pious Muslims and has to a great degree influenced the Muslim culture. The greeting that Muhammad taught Muslims to offer each other, "may peace be upon you" (Arabic: *as-salamu 'alaykum*) is used by Muslims throughout the world. Many details of major Islamic rituals such as daily prayers, the fasting and the annual pilgrimage are only found in the Sunnah and not the Quran. Muslims have traditionally expressed love and veneration for Muhammad. Stories of Muhammad's life, his intercession and of his miracles have permeated popular Muslim thought and poetry Among Arabic odes to Muhammad, Qasidat al-Burda ("Poem of the Mantle") by the Egyptian Sufi al-Busiri (1211–1294) is particularly well-known, and widely held to possess a healing, spiritual power. The Quran refers to Muhammad as "a mercy (*rahmat*) to the worlds" (Quran 21:107).

The association of rain with mercy in Oriental countries has led to imagining Muhammad as a rain cloud dispensing blessings and stretching over lands, reviving the dead hearts, just as rain revives the seemingly dead earth (see, for example, the Sindhi poem of Shah 'Abd al-Latif).

Muhammad's birthday is celebrated as a major feast throughout the Islamic world, excluding Wahhabi-dominated Saudi Arabia where these public celebrations are discouraged. When Muslims say or write the name of Muhammad, they usually follow it with the Arabic phrase *ṣallā llahu 'alayhi wa-sallam* (*may God honor him and grant him peace*) or the English phrase *peace be upon him*.

In casual writing, the abbreviations SAW (for the Arabic phrase) or PBUH (for the English phrase) are sometimes used; in printed matter, a small calligraphic rendition is commonly used (ﷺ).

Sufism

The Sunnah contributed much to the development of Islamic law, particularly from the end of the first Islamic century. Muslim mystics, known as sufis, who were seeking for the inner meaning of the Quran and the inner nature of Muhammad, viewed the prophet of Islam not only as a prophet but also as a perfect human being. All Sufi orders trace their chain of spiritual descent back to Muhammad.

What Is Islam

What is the meaning of the word 'Islam'?

Islam is made up of words and words. Salam is an Arabic word, the meaning of this word is dedicated to God, that is, the word Islam itself means, the person who surrenders to God, he is a believer of Islam religion.

Muhammad was a follower of Lord Shiva and was devotee of Buddha's thoughts and Technology of Lord Shiva.

Muhammad was a devoted to women and to increase his wealth, he did 13 marriages. Due to which his business is flourishing till date. Those who wrote the Quran had also studied the Gita, and were influenced by chapter number 12 (which is to offer oneself to God by adopting the path of devotion). By making rules for the followers engaged in his business, he gave the name of Quran, which teaches to be devoted to women for business. Muhammad is inspired to surrender (Islam).

According to Islamic belief, he was a prophet and messenger of God, also known as the Prophet of Islam, sent to present and confirm the monotheistic teachings first preached by Adam, Abraham, Moses, Jesus, and other prophets. were. Islam is an Abrahamic sect, a monotheistic sect derived from apostolic tradition. According to tradition, the beginning of its last apostle is in the Arabian Peninsula of the 7th century.

According to Islamic tradition, the incarnated book transmitted to humans by Muhammad, the last prophet of Allah, is based on the teachings of the Qur'an, and includes Hadith, Seerat un-Nabi and Shari'a texts.

Sunni, Shia, Sufi and Ahmadiyya communities are prominent in Islam. The religious places of Islam are called mosques.

There are five basic pillars of Islam.

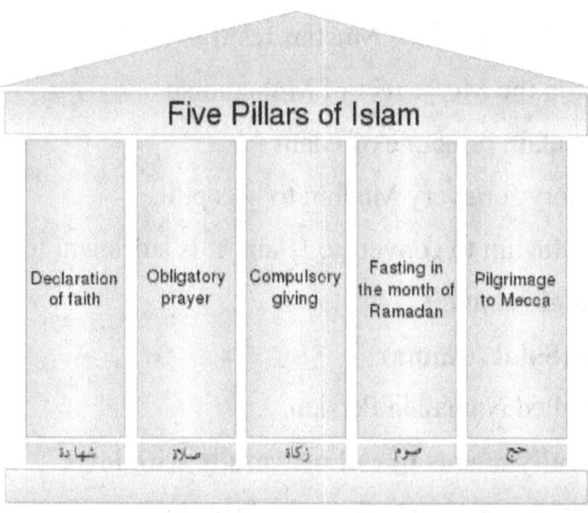

Five duties are necessary to become a good man (Muslim). ccording to the belief of Muslims, there are five basic pillars or Farz of Islam religion, which is considered by every Muslim to be the basic idea of his life.

These things are told in the famous hadith "Hadith e Jibril".

edit five columns

1. Shahada

2. salat or prayer

3. Saum or Roza

4. Zakat

5. Hajj

Sunni,Sufi and Ahmadiyya group has 5 pillars and Shia has 6 pillars and 6th pillar is as **IMAN**

I. To be a witness (Shahada)-

This literally means to bear witness.

In Islam it means this Arabic declaration-

La ilaha illallah Muhammad Rasool Allah.

There is no other God but Allah and Muhammad is the Messenger (Apostle) of Allah.

By this declaration every Muslim testifies to the monotheism of God and his belief in the Messenger of Muhammad.

This is the main principle of Islam.

It is obligatory for every Muslim to accept it.

For a non-Muslim to convert to Islam, it is sufficient to admit it before an Islamic religious judge.

II. Prayer (Salat / Namaz) -

It is also called Namaz in Persian.

Aajan literally means to call peacefully with love.

And Namaz means to pray from the heart in peace.

In Islam, there are five obligations on every Muslim, which are necessary on every Muslim, that is, it is a duty.

There is a law for a Muslim to offer prayers five times per day.

Namaz-e-Fajr (Dawn Prayer) - This is the first prayer that is offered in the morning before the sun rises.

Namaz-e-Zuhr (Eternal Prayer) This is the second prayer which is offered after the sun sets in the mid-day.

Namaz-e-Asr (daytime prayer)- This is the third prayer which takes place shortly before the setting of the sun.

Namaz-e-Maghrib (Evening Prayer) - The fourth prayer which takes place immediately after sunset.

Namaz-e-Isha (Night Prayer) - The last fifth prayer which is offered one and a half hours after sunset

It literally means praying from the heart and in the heart.

Which is written in Arabic language to read the mind by a special rule.

According to Islam, prayer is the gratitude of man towards God.

Method to Perform Namaz

1.   Perform BAJJU without any Mantra Chanting.

2.   Sit down on Vajrasana.

3.   Watch both hands together.

4.   Perform Shiva Surrender Pranayam/Naman Pranayam.

Methods are to take the deep Breathing in sitting position and watch the both joined hand and outhale the breathing and bring head to earth and hand to be forward.

5.   Perform 21 to 108 times

6.   Sit down Peacefully.

7.   Do not Chant any Mantra in all this process.

III. Saum or Roza-

Method to Perform ROJA

Basic Meaning of ROJA is sitting in one place peacefully without food and water.

1.   Morning 3am to 4am - Perform Sarghi with Fruit if available.

2.   Sit down in Vipassana Meditation from 4am to till sunset.

3.   Perform Namaz and take Satvik Food .

4.   Perform Vipassana till 9 pm and rest at night.

5.   Perform 40 days continuously and end on Dwitya and perform IDD.

IV. Zakat-

- Zakat is a religious obligation, ordering all Muslims who meet the necessary criteria to donate a certain portion of wealth each year to charitable causes.

- Zakat is said to purify yearly earnings that are over and above what is required to provide the essential needs of a person or family.

- Zakat is based on income and the value of possessions. The common minimum amount for those who qualify is 2.5%, or 1/40 of a Muslim's total savings and wealth.

- If personal wealth is below the Nisab **(the minimum amount that a Muslim must have before being obliged to give zakat)** during one lunar year, no zakat is owed for that period.

V. Hajj-

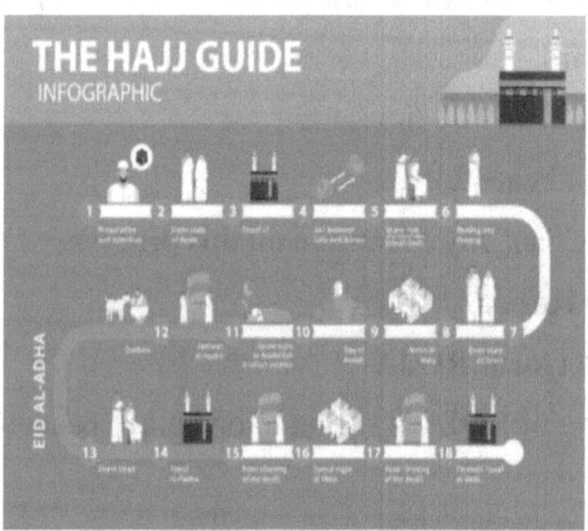

Hajj is a pilgrimage that Muslims from all around the world should perform once in their whole life. Hajj is performed for five days, from 8th to 12th Dhul-Hijjah. Before you start your journey of Hajj, you must learn the whole process.

Kinds of Hajj

There are three main kinds of Hajj.

A. Hajj al-Ifrad

This kind of Hajj refers to fulfilling the rituals, and there is no need to sacrifice animals or do Qurbani. It involves only wearing Ihram for the Hajj and removing it only on the day of sacrifice. **Mufrid** is the name given to a pilgrim who performs this kind of Hajj.

B. Hajj al-Tamattu

It is the most popular form of Hajj, and it is the one that Prophet Muhammed (PBUH) urged his companions to follow. People from other countries usually practice Hajj al-Tamattu in Saudi Arabia.

It applies to conducting Umrah ceremonies during the Hajj season and then completing the Hajj steps between the eighth and thirteenth days of Dhu al-Hijjah.

Muttamatti is the name for a pilgrim who performs this kind of Hajj. It requires the sacrifice of a sacrificial animal.

C. Hajj al-Qiran

In Qiran, one must stick to the Ihram restrictions. It refers to wearing Ihram for both Umrah and Hajj and not taking it off before the day of sacrifice in Mina.

This type necessarily requires a sacrificial animal to complete the rituals. **Qaarin** is the name for a pilgrim who performs this kind of Hajj.

A step by step guide on how Muslims perform Hajj

It can be done in various ways, and there are many schools of Islamic thought with their own set of scholarly differences.**Before Arriving Makkah**

Step 1: Making Intention (Niyah)

It's critical to make your Niyah in your heart before arriving in Makkah to start Hajj.

The process that Muslim men or women have to perform is explained here. These steps are crucial and are considered necessary before performing Hajj.

1. Perform ablutions (Cleaning the body so that Muslims attain the physical purity of their bodies. This process involves some mandatory and other functions).

2. Perform Ghusl.

3. Apply perfume, trim the head & beard.

4. Clipp of your finger & toenails

5. Trimming of the mustache

6. Shaving off body hairs (So that during Hajj, you are not allowed to do so).

7. Wearing Ihram (two pieces of white sheets, namely Izar and Rida for men and for women simple light color clothes. Both men and women should wear sandals that should expose the middle bones of your midfoot).

8. Perform two Rakats of Salah al-Ihram. The head must be covered in it.

9. Pronounce Niyyah as Muslims approach the Miqat.

10. Reciting Talbiyah. As you have now entered the sacred boundary of the Khana e Kabba after Miqat.

11. This recitation of Talbiyah must be continued until the commencement of Tawaf.

12. Then onto the next stage of traveling to Mecca. It is considered the next step of performing Umrah.

When you arrive at Makkah's holiest Masjid al-Haram, you'll be able to start the most important spiritual journey of your life. It is vital to follow each action following the Holy Prophet's Sunnah (P.B.U.H). In truth, following all processes in the Holy Prophet's (P.B.U.H) exact order is also needed.**mrahAfter Arriving Makkah** When you arrive in Makkah, you will perform Umrah, which includes Tawaf and Sa'i. Umrah provides Muslims with a chance to renew their religion, accept forgiveness, and pray for their needs.

Step 2: Tawaf

Tawaf is one of the essential pilgrimage rituals, and it entails walking in anti-clockwise circles around the Kaaba. A Tawaf is made up of seven circuits, each of which begins and ends at the black stone. You can make voluntary prayers in addition to your Tawaf to thank Allah (SWT) for your safe arrival and to continue this unique spiritual journey.

Step 3: Sa'i

When you have done Tawaf, you will do Sa'i, which involves walking and running between Safa and Marwa's two hills. You'll start the Sa'i on Safa and walk towards Marwa until you see the green sign. When you've completed seven laps between Safa and Marwa, your Sa'i is finished. Men will have their hair trimmed or shaved after Sa'i, while women will have their hair clipped to the end of their fingertip. Your Umrah is now complete, now you are allowed to leave Ihram before the 8th of Dhul Hijjah.**st Day of Hajj**

DAY-I Tarwiyah Day (8th Dhul Hijjah)

After the Maghrib prayer of 7th Dhul-Hijjah, the date 8 Dhul-Hijjah begins. In those late-night hours, try to complete all Hajj preparations. Pilgrims wear the Ihram and declare their Niyah to perform the pilgrimage. Men cover their heads and offer two Rakahs of Nafal for Ihram in the Haram Sharif. Men are no longer allowed to cover their heads during Ihram after this stage.

Step 4: Miqat

When reaching the outer boundary of Mecca, known as Miqat, the first ritual of Hajj is entering Ihram, a pilgrim's holy state. Before they can enter Makkah, they must pass through five Mawaqeet. Allah Almighty declared that anybody wishing to perform Hajj or Umrah at His glorified House should enter the state of Ihram from particular locations where he is not allowed to pass without Ihram. Before leaving for Makkah, they shower, put on their Ihram, which means wearing simple clothes – two unstitched clothes for men or loose-fitting clothing for women and make the niyyah perform the Hajj.

They begin to make Talbiyah:

"Here I am, O Allah, here I am, here I am. You have no partner; here I am. Verily all praise and blessings are Yours and all sovereignty. You have no partner."

Step 5: Proceed to Mina

The pilgrims then set out in large groups from Mecca to the vast tent-city of Mina, either on foot or by bus or vehicle. It's an 8-kilometer walk. They will stay in Mina for the whole day. There are no significant rituals performed on the first night, so pilgrims pass their time praying.

You have to set the tent when you arrive in Mina. You will pray dhuhr, asr, maghrib, isha, and Fajr here, reducing your four unit prayers to 2 parts each, as prescribed by the Quran. Spend the night praying to Allah (SWT), reading the Qur'an, and getting ready for the next day. It's a rare night for spiritual remembrance and commitment.**nd Day of Hajj**

DAY-II Day of Arafah (9th Dhul Hijjah):

The second day starts on 9th Dhul-Hijjah.

Step 6: Arafah

The Day of Arafat is one of the most important days in the Islamic calendar, not only for Hajj. The final sermon of Prophet Muhammad was delivered on Mount Mercy in Arafat. Pilgrims spend the day hereafter traveling 14.4 kilometers from Mina. Pilgrims spend this time saying Talbiyah, saying Darud Sharif, and reciting all of the Dua's in Arabic and their native language. It is preferable to perform Waquf while standing, but sitting is also appropriate.

Pilgrims move to nearby Mount Arafat on the second day of Hajj. Pilgrims offer Dhuhr and Asr and remain there until the sun sets, and praying for His grace and mercy.

The imam of Masjid-e-Namrah leads mixed and simplified Zuhr and Asr prayers at Zuhr time with one adhan but different iqamahs. Most Muslims around the world prefer to fast on this day. After sunset, pilgrims travel 9 kilometers north of Arafat to Muzdalifah, where they spend the night.

Step 7: Muzdalifah

You'll leave Arafah after sunset and go to Muzdalifah, the open plain area between Mina and Arafat. When you arrive in Muzdalifah, offer your Salah of maghrib and Isha one after the other, minimizing the Isha salah to two Rakat. Many people can start gathering pebbles here for tomorrow's rituals, then leave just before sunrise.

It is a very blessed night to praise Allah, recite Darud Sharif, read the Quran, say Talbiyah, and humbly supplicate. You should either pray or rest for the night. The Prophet (SAW) slept until just before Fajr instead of participating in night worship as he usually did.

You should also pick pebbles when in Muzdalifah to do Rami [the devil's stoning] for the next three days. The stones can be roughly the same size. You need to pick up 21 pebbles but as a precautionary measure, bring the total to 70. You will miss the target or see any pebbles fall from your hand as you go through the process of throwing the stones at the Jamarat. Pebbles can be found almost anywhere in Mina. When the sun is about to rise, start your journey Mina.**d Day of Hajj**

DAY-III First day of Eid (10th Dhul Hijjah):

You will leave Muzdalifah after performing Fajr salah and go to Mina. Do remember to recite the Talbiyah. The day known as Yawm-ul-Hajj, or the Day of Sacrifice, falls on the 10th of Dhul Hijjah.

Step 8: The Rami

Pilgrims return to Mina before sunrise to participate in a ritual that represents stoning the devil. It is the longest and most risky day of the Hajj for all pilgrims when millions of people throw pebbles at the pillars. Rami is an activity of throwing pebbles at the Jamarat. Thousands of pilgrims gather on the Jamarat Bridge, that has the three devil-like pillars, to re-enact the event.

Rami's ritual was a representation of Ibrahim's (AS) acts when he was ordered to kill his son, Ismail (AS), in response to Allah's direction (SWT). The devil tried to stop Him, but He threw some pebbles on the devil. Pilgrims throw seven consecutive small stones at the Jamrat Al-

Aqabah, a rare stone monument. When you arrive in Jamarat, go to Jamarat al-Aqaba, the giant pillar, and throw the first seven pebbles there. Every time you throw the pebbles, say Takbir اللہ اکبَر □ʾ(Allah is The Greatest).

Step 9: Animal Sacrifice (Qurbani)

On the 10th, 11th, or 12th day, Pilgrims sacrifice animals at any time. Pilgrims must either slaughter a sheep, cow, goats, or camel themselves or pay for it to be performed in their honor. This rite reflects Prophet Ibrahim's willingness to sacrifice his son before being replaced by a lamb, and it represents the believers' devotion to God. It is appropriate to give an animal sacrifice to God after the stoning ceremony. Each pilgrim used to do this independently, but nowadays, it is much more popular for pilgrims to buy a sacrifice voucher. Many will then go to Mecca to conduct Tawaf and Sa'ee, which involves seven times circling the Kaaba and running between Safa and Marwa's hills.

Step 10: Halq

Pilgrims trim or shave their hair (men only) and remove their Ihram clothing at this stage. It is better to cut one's hair like the Prophet Muhammad (SAW) did. Women trim her hair to a fingertip's length.

Step 11: Tawaf-e-Ziarat

As part of your Hajj rites, you can now go to Makkah to conduct Tawaf al-ifadha and Sa'i. The Tawaf al-ifada and Sa'i are needed. Both must be done after the Rami, sacrifice, and head trimming, according to the Sunnah. Its practice is identical to that of Tawaf of Umrah. It can be done at any time of day or night, from the 10th of Zil Hijjah until the 12th of Zil Hijjah sunset.**h Day of Hajj**

DAY-IV Second day of Eid (11th Dhul Hijjah):

You'll have your 21 pebbles ready on the 11th of Dhul Hijjah afternoon.

Step 12: Rami of Jamrarat

If anyone wants to leave Mina, they have to throw the pebbles on the 12th day and go before sunset. If the sun sets before he leaves, he will now have to stay in Mina for the third night. Believers return to Mina for three nights and start throwing stones on each of the three Jamarat. Rami usually is accessible in the evenings or before nighttime. Pilgrims will now spend the next two to three days in Mina, completing their pilgrimage's most challenging part.

Step 13: Supplicate, Zikr and Ibadah

With your raised hand and facing Qibla, praise Allah and recite Duas in Arabic or supplicate in your own words. You will ask Allah whatever you want as long as you do not commit any sins.

h Day of Hajj

DAY-V Third day of Eid (12th Dhul Hijjah):

The Hajj completes on the 12 Dhul Hijjah, the final day of the Hajj.

Step 14: Rami of Jamarat

On the 5th day, pilgrims throw seven stones on pillars once more after Zawal. Start with Jamarah al-Ula, then Jamarah al-Wusta, and then Jamrah al-Aqaba. You have to stone each one with seven pebbles in a row. The pilgrims then spend the next two to three days in Mina praying and remembering Allah.

Step 15: Final chance for Tawaf-e-Ziarat

You have the choice of moving to Makkah before sunset after today's Rami. If you were unable to do Tawaf-e-Ziarah earlier, you have to do so today before Maghrib. Pilgrims must perform the Tawaf and Sa'e rites at the Kaaba and surrounding hills. The rites are conducted similarly during the Umrah, although it is highly advised that these rites are performed only after the stoning, sacrifice, and hair-cutting rituals.

Step 16: Tawaf al-Wida

The farewell Tawaf is the last rite we do before leaving Makkah. It is wajib and must be done before leaving the Haram's borders. In Islam, it is not permissible to skip this Tawaf unless there is a reasonable cause. You will complete seven Tawaf laps with this Tawaf. After that, offer two Rakats of salah and drink water (zam zam). After this Tawaf, there is no Sa'i or head-shaving or trimming.

Conclusion

Before returning home, many pilgrims visit Medina, Islam's second holiest city, where the Prophet Muhammad and his closest companions are buried. Visiting Medina, on the other hand, is not included in the pilgrimage. Adult Muslims who have the financial resources must perform Hajj at least once in their lives to demonstrate their faith and devotion to Allah Almighty. Muslims must learn how to follow the Hajj rituals step by step. UrduPoint presented you a complete and easy step-by-step guide to perform Hajj so that you learn it before you go on this religious journey. We hope our guide will help you a lot in performing Hajj.

DRAWBACKS IN ISLAM-

In Islam reciting the Quran is danger as this book is not a researched book,this book is written by the people to collect the data before 1400 which is against of present Socio and political condition.

Following drawback is as under.-

1. The person who is not following the Quran, they are KAFIR.KAFIR must be killed.

2. Polygamy is the tradition.Gents may have 4 wife but not Women.

3. Gents torturing the Women,even Incharge of Masjid also instructing to punish the Women.

4. Three Talaq is common,after three Talaq,Women with children are removed from the House.

5. Marriage is in close relatives causing disorder in children.

6. Sunnat and Khatna to Boy and girl respectively- Removing the skin from Pennis in boy childhood and removing skin from vagina in girl childhood is dangerous even if few children die also.

7. Parda Pratha is dangerous for the present condition.

8. Mutah Marriage is dangerous for the Society.

9. Wrong method of prayer and Roja is dangerous for health.

10. Marriage of Maulvi,Maulana,Imam is dangerous for society.

11. This OLD IDEOLOGY was not re-written in the last 1400 years and is dangerous for World.

12. This old Ideology book which is only recited by the Muslim is producing the Demon nature people.

13. Girls marriage age is 12 year.

14. In the Namaj Session Maulvi had political talk against KAFIR,Society and Politics causing disturbances in Society.

15. No control on producing children.

Merit- Rejecting to drink wine and People accepting BEBA WOMEN in community freely is the merit of this community.

Buddhism

Technology of Anapana Meditation,Vipassana,Mangal Maitri and Buddha Dhamma

BUDDHISM-Lord Budha followed the Geeta and practiced the Chapter-3,6,7,8,12,13,14,15,16,17 & 18 and as per social condition he himself taught the practical view of above Chapters for 45 year and he changed the social condition of World.His Chanting Mantra is-

Buddham Saranam Gacchami, Dhammam Saranam Gachhami, Shangham Saranam Gachhami.

To become healthy (To control of Lust,anger and Greed) and free from material attachment in all respect, Main Teaching is of strictly follow the Ayurvedic lifestyle, Perform Panch sheel/Eight Sheel, Anapana Meditation,Vipassana Technology and Mangal Maitri/Positivity to enrich the Yagya (Sacrifice), Dana (Charity) and Tapasya (austerities or penances.)

Technology of Anapan

My Breath and I

Anapan is the first step in the practice of Vipassana meditation. Anapana means observation of natural, normal respiration, as it comes in and as it goes out.

It is an easy to learn, objective and scientific technique that helps develop concentration of the mind. Observation of the breath is the ideal object for meditation because it is always available and it is completely non-sectarian. Anapan is very different from techniques that are based on the artificial regulation of breath.

There are no rites or rituals involved in the practice or presentation of Anapana. Anapana provides a tool to deal with the fears, anxieties and pressures across all age groups. Besides helping to calm and concentrate the mind, Anapana help people to understand themselves better and gives them an insight into the workings of their own minds.Because of its simplicity, the technique is easy to understand and practice.

The SAMADHI

The word can be broken down as sam, "together" or "integrated"; ā, "towards"; dhā, "to get, to hold": "to acquire integration or wholeness, or truth" A blissful super consciousness state in which a yogi perceives the identity of the individualized Soul and Cosmic Spirit. Samadhi is often achieved through meditation. In this state, the three aspects of meditation—meditator, an act of meditation, the object of meditation known as God—are finally united. Samadhi is regarded as the climax of all spiritual and intellectual activity. The power to attain Samadhi is a precondition of attaining release from the cycle of death and rebirth (samsara). Hence, the death of a person having this power is also considered a samadhi.

Maharishi Patanjali has elaborated eight limbs of yoga in his book Yoga Sutras as:
1. Yam (Observances)
2. Niyama (Abstinences)
3. Asana (Postures)
4. Pranayam (Breath controlling)
5. Pratyahara (Withdrawal of senses)
6. Dharana (Determination)
7. Dhyana (Meditation)
8. Samadhi (Self-realization or Nirvana as per Budha Technology).

Stages of Samadhi

Samprajnata Samadhi (Savikalpa)

The first level of samadhi is where you are peaceful, quiet, in meditation but you are available to the outside world. In this state, you are sitting quietly, consciously getting rid of disturbances of your mind and meditating. If some stimulus happens, you use your prajna (knowledge) to respond; that is the Samprajnata Samadhi. Savikalpa samadhi is a state of conditioned oneness. The meditator experiences the merging of his soul with infinite consciousness; however, he cannot preserve the experience outside of meditation. It is simply an experience of meditativeness. For a short period of time, you lose all human consciousness. In this state, the concepts of time and space are different than in material nature. However, this is not yet a permanent state and everybody has to return to ordinary consciousness. Patanjali describes the four stages of Savikalpa Samadhi are possible.

1. Savitarka Samadhi

This means "thought transformation on an object with the help of words." Perhaps it is because so much of the everyday mind's processes, including words, remain intact in this level of samadhi that many meditators do not recognize that they have in fact experienced Samadhi. It's the stage of gaining knowledge. "Knowledge," in yogic terms, always carries a sense of distinguishing the real from the unreal. In this stage, our thoughts transform into an object with the help of words and start a dialogue which is called Tarka. In the state of Savitarka Samadhi, the mind weigh things with awareness and decides whether they are useful to discuss or not.

2. Sa-Asmita Samadhi

This is the final stage of Savitarka Samadhi. When the yogi becomes established in the one-pointed state of consciousness achieved in sananda samadhi the mind becomes even more purified, and is able to penetrate deeper. Even the ahankara, or ego-sense—despite its power, its pervasive nature, and its seeming solidity—is only a vritti, a single thought of individualized existence. This vritti too can be suppressed, and when this happens the yogi can directly perceive the source of the ahankara: the mahat.

3. Savichara Samadhi

"The state of samadhi concerned with subtle objects extends up to Prakriti, the source of all manifestation." As savichara samadhi deepens, the yogi may begin to develop an understanding of the true nature of time and space and may also gain knowledge of certain aspects of the mahat, or cosmic mind. The mind (buddhi) experiences and explores the subtler level of the object through an alteration of awareness between its spatial, temporal, and causal aspects. After some practice, the yogi will be able to fully transfer consciousness from the vitarka to the vicara level. Savichara Samadhi is a state of silence in which thinking is available, but the mind is quiet.

4. Sa-Ananda Samadhi

Here the mind is devoid of the objective world, you move beyond the intellect. There is no reasoning or reflection, just the tranquility of the settled mind. The sattvic (pure) mind is only aware of its own joy. The focus is on the inner powers of perception and within the mind itself. It's known as a "blissful" Samadhi filled with joyful peace.

Asamprajnata Samadhi (Nirvikalpa)

The second level of Samadhi is when you go deeper into yourself, away from the world outside and if some stimulus happens, it won't affect you. This is Asamprajnata Samadhi. In Mahabharata, Arjuna is supposed to have practiced his archery with such concentration. The only thing present at this stage is pure, empty consciousness: only a self-aware being. This is Nirvikalpa or Nirbija samadhi. The mind of the yogi who attains to take on some of the omniscient and omnipotent qualities of the cosmic. The yogi who is able to navigate this stage eventually attains discriminative wisdom and perfect purity of mind and surrenders all attachments.

5. Nirvichara Samadhi

It refers to the state in which the mental alternations of shabda, artha, and jñana are suspended. The less-real components, shabda and jñana, fall away completely, while the mind is absorbed in only artha, or form, and loses its awareness of being the knower.

It's where we have greater control over the mind, ideas, intellect, and dialogues. The memory about the nature of the object (its identifying sound and the accumulated knowledge) are temporarily transcended during Nirvitarka samadhi.

6. Nirvichara Samadhi

For the first time, true one-pointed concentration becomes possible. Even subtle thoughts do not occur. The perceptual limitations of time and space are transcended; this state is called Nirvichara Samadhi.

7. Kaivalya Samadhi

The final stage is to reach Kaivalya Samadhi: complete, final, and eternal union with the real, eternal form.

VIPASSANA- 'Vipassana meditation practice' is the most popular meditation practice in the whole world these days under the Second

Buddha's rule. The pure public and scientific teaching of Lord Tathagata Samyak Sambuddha is prevalent in the whole world today in the name of Vipassana. This is an experimental meditation method. It can be known, understood and benefited only by using itself.

Whether Vipassana is the teaching of Lord Buddha or not:

Scholars around the world see the teachings of Lord Buddha divided into three parts, that is-

I. Pariyatti (the theoretical side),

II. Patipatti (the practical side) and

III. Pativedan (that is, to see the truth in pieces or pierce).

Vipassana is the practical side of the teachings of the Lord. Worth a try yourself. Qualified for an interview. Effective immediately. He is going to make further progress on the path of Dhamma.

Vipassana's return to India

Vipassana flourished in ancient India and also went to many countries of the world. Due to the practical people started to perform puja to Budha in India, after 1000-1500 years, Vipassana slowly ended.

By the time of the medieval period people forgot its name.

In neighboring countries it continued purely in some parts.

Particularly in Myanmar (Burma), the guru-shishya tradition was prevalent. This priceless learning came again in 1969 through Satyanarayan Goenka ji, a disciple of the householder Acharya Uba Khin.

About 2500 years after the parinirvana of Lord Buddha, it again appeared in India.

Vipassana in different parts of India

At present, the cycle of Vipassana has started again and it is rapidly going to almost every corner of the country and doing welfare for the people. About 1000 assistants and senior teachers are basically giving training in about more than 300 centers for the propagation of Vipassana. Seeing the teachings of Buddha again in India in its pure, universal and scientific form gives great relief to Indians. It is only through this knowledge that they can understand and understand the Buddha's revolution in the right form.

Vipassana in most countries of the world

Now Vipassana has spread to most parts of the world. America, UK, Australia, New Zealand, France, Germany, Canada, Italy, Mongolia, Spain, Japan, Thailand, Taiwan, Cambodia, Sri Lanka Burma, Nepal etc. countries besides Dubai, Muscat, Lebanon, Iran, Far China, In countries like Korea, Pakistan etc. Vipassana is also taught through centers.

Role of Vipassana Acharya Satyanarayan Goenka

Many works were done by Pujya Vishwa Vipassanaacharya Goenka ji by establishing 'Vipassana Vishwa Vidyapeeth' in 1977 at a place named Igatpuri near Mumbai. According to the increasing demand, training centers were opened all over India. Assistant Teachers were appointed. Continuous publication of Vipassana monthly magazine, creation and publication of ancient Buddhist literature and new literature. Visits to Buddhist countries, visits to ancient Buddhist sites of India and establishment of centers etc. Many researches have also been done on Vipassana.

Research work through Vipassana Vidhyana Vipassana

Planning for publication of Tripitakas of original Buddhist literature through Vipassana Research Institute in Mumbai, Organizing many lectures in India and abroad, Revered Guruji's famous speech at UNO, Steps towards world peace, Vipassana in governance, in all religious communities Many works were done to spread the teachings of Buddha etc. Vipassana Videshna Vinayak is playing an active role in this.

Through this, all facilities for scientific research on parity, literary subjects are available.

Buddha's teaching to all classes and classes

Vipassana Vidya, reinvented by Lord Gautam Buddha, is a completely non-sectarian method.

Today, when so much anarchy is spread in the name of religion, this sectarian-less education acts as a beacon of light even in the darkest of darkness.

People of all sects come to learn this lore - be it male or female, child, old, young people of all ages come.

There are some people of very high education and also very illiterate people.

The rich also come and the poor also come.

Government, non-government officials and employees and traders, industrialists from all walks of life also come.

Therefore, it will not be an exaggeration to say that people from all walks of life come to learn Vipassana.

Vipassana Refinement and Pali Language

Nowadays online and full-time training is also given through Vipassana Dhyana Vinyasa.

This is a certificate course.

In this course, the Pali language and its grammar are exposed.

Along with this, some sutras of Tripitaka are also practiced.

The duration of the course is 6 months.

In this, there is a practice class of one and a half hours every Saturday evening and on Sunday morning.

The applicant must have passed at least one ten-day Vipassana course and 12th standard.

Therefore, Dhammitras, we can say that through Vipassana sadhana, the doors have been opened for all classes of people through the basic teachings of Lord Buddha and very important steps have been taken in the direction of propagation of Buddha's speech and words.

Vipassana inspires people to work with a calm, pure, pure mind. It makes the seeker more active than before. Good luck to all...!

Mangal Friendship

Hello friends! Today I would like to talk to you about Mangal Maitri. I you have read my earlier articles, then you must have noticed that I always talk about **Mangal Maitri** . This question will be in your mind that what is Mangal Friendship and how to do it. That's why today I am going to tell you about this.

What is Mangal Friendship?

In the meditation method taught by Gautam Buddha, **"Vipassana"** , there is great importance of friendship. After meditating in this method, when the mind becomes pure and feels happy, then we distribute this purity, purity, happiness among all beings, deities, worshiped persons. And wish all of them good luck. Mangal friendship is done for 5 minutes after meditation.

How to do Mangal Friendship?

Stabilizing the mind and filling it with happiness, wishing good luck to all beings, living beings, living and nonliving, deities, auspicious and inauspicious powers and whoever is in this universe. May all be happy, be happy, follow modesty and morality, wish everyone good, good luck to all, wish for everyone's welfare.

Befriend oneself

Sometimes we ourselves are disappointed, sad and in trouble. So unless we ourselves are pure chit, happy, how will we see others on Mars? How will you wish for someone else's happiness? Therefore, when our mind is sad about something, then first of all we should make good friendships for ourselves. May I be happy, may I remain a still picture, may I be happy, may my mind be calm, steady and intelligent, I should not quarrel with anyone.

No one bothers me.

I live a life of modesty.

In this way, make good friends for yourself.

When to do Mangal Maitri?

After 20 minutes of meditation in the morning, do Mangal Maitri for 5 minutes. Whenever the mind is happy during the day, distribute that happiness among all.

Do Mars with a steady mind.

Benefits of Mars Friendship

- The mind is pure
- Hatred goes away
- Enemies also become friends
- Good health
- Enjoy living life
- Creates a positive environment

Friendship Sutra - What are the eleven qualities of friendship?

Lord Tathagata Samyak Sambuddha narrated this friendship formula for the benefit of all the people –

Bhikkhu Ananda says – I have heard that. Once upon a time Lord Buddha used to reside in Jetavanarama of Anathapindak in Shravasti town.

Addressing the monks there, he said 'Monks!'

The monks also replied to the Lord by saying Bhadanta.

The Lord said – monks – Eleven takes to practice, increase, repeat, practice, increase, repeat, engage like a connected vehicle, be like an object in the base, establish, increase acquaintance and become well practiced.

There are qualities. Which eleven? So these are as follows-

Eleven qualities of friendship

> ➤ The one who makes friends sleeps peacefully.
> ➤ Live happily.
> ➤ Never had a bad dream.
> ➤ Loved by humans.
> ➤ He is dear to humans also.
> ➤ The gods protect him.
> ➤ He is not harmed by fire, poison or weapons.
> ➤ His mind quickly becomes samadhi (concentrated).
> ➤ His form shines.
> ➤ He gives up his life consciously.
> ➤ He has goodness.

This is how Lord Buddha explained to the monks.

Friendship, Chitta Vimukti should be practiced again and again. Like a connected vehicle, one should be engaged in the feeling of friendship. Friendship should remain like a thing in its base form. Must be firmly installed. One should increase the introduction and get used to it well. In this, those who have a feeling of friendship get the above eleven qualities. All those monks greeted the voice of the Lord with a happy heart.

Good luck everyone!

Say Dhamma or say Dharma!

In the present time, there is a lot of discussion on the words 'Dhamma' and 'Dharma'. Especially many people like to call Buddha words not

'Dharma' but 'Dhamma'. Is there any difference or difference of meaning between these two words?

In this article, we will try to understand this. The word Dhamma is found in ancient India only 2600 years ago or earlier. Nowadays, instead of this word, only religion is found in Hindi. The meaning of the word religion is taken from a particular sect. Like Hindu, Muslim, Jain, Buddhist, Sikh, Christian etc. On knowing more deeply, it is known that such and such sects, creeds, rituals, customs, costumes, philosophical beliefs, scriptures-books, Teej-festivals, festivals, food-drinks, tilak- Signs or symbols etc. are considered as religious symbols or traditions.

Whereas in ancient times, 'Dhamma' meant the laws of nature, the laws of nature, the law of the world or the law of the world was called 'Dhamma', that is, the law of nature or the law of nature which applies equally to all beings of the world without any discrimination.

It is the same Dhamma. The form of religion which is always universal, universal, universal or everlasting.

It is eternal. Molecules that hold molecules and those that hold particles. Which is simple, natural, easy. That is the 'Dhamma'.

Now if we do a comparative study of the prevailing meaning and real nature of the word religion, then it will be known that religion i.e. 'Sampradaya' is the real enemy of Dhamma.

'Sampradaya' has nothing to do with Dhamma. He always makes the Dhamma secondary and narrow, hence it is also nonsensical. Therefore, while explaining Dharma or Dhamma, Vipassana Acharya Goenka ji has rightly said- Religion is neither Hindu Buddhist, nor Muslim Jainism.

Dhamma purity of mind, Dharma peace and happiness. According to the ancient definition of Dhamma, he can be both skilled or unskilled.

That's why gradually, efficient deeds, that is, only virtuous deeds, came to be called religion. And unskilled deeds came to be called adharma.

But basically Dharma or Dhamma was nature.

Good or bad, skilled or unskilled, Arya (superior) or non-Arya, Punya or Papakarma means both natures. Whatever we wear is Dharma or Dhamma. Then the result can be equally good or bad.

Therefore in short it can be said that Dhamma and Dharma, despite being similar, have become different nowadays.

Religion has become a cult.

It has become secondary.

Therefore, as ideal Buddhists, we should wear Buddha's words by knowing and understanding them in the right sense. Namo Buddhay.

Buddha says - God is nowhere to be found, don't waste your time and energy searching for Him.

Difference between Dharma and Dhamma

- In religion you cannot speak against God, you cannot disobey the scriptures, you cannot use your intelligence. Whereas in the Dhamma, there is a teaching to test oneself and use one's intellect.*

- Religion says that some power like so-called God will come to do your good.

- Whereas the Dhamma says – Atta Deep Bhava means be your own lamp.

- The Buddha also says: "I am neither the liberator, nor am I the giver of salvation. I'm just going to show you the way. Dhamma means the highest humanistic basis for living life.

- Many people would believe that Dharma and Dhamma are one and the same. They need to be analyzed. One has to take birth in

Dharma, while one has to receive (education) in Dhamma. which anyone can get.

- Buddha told his followers that there are illogical things in religion. E.g. soul, paramatma, ghost, god, deities etc. Whereas Dhamma is based on scientific point of view. The Dhamma gives priority to logic and intelligence. That's why he rejects God.

- There is inequality in religion, there is discrimination, there is high and low. Whereas in Dhamma all is one. All are equal. There is no discrimination. Dhamma is a teaching, a knowledge, which is for all. There is division in religion. Rights are divided into classes. Whereas there is classlessness in the Dhamma. Rights and knowledge are for all.

- In religion, some call Brahma the creator of the universe, while some call themselves the messenger of God. Whereas the one who taught Dhamma did not describe himself as a messenger of God, but described himself as a man showing the true path.

- * Tathagata Gautam Buddha, giving the meaning of 'Buddha', says: "Buddha" is the name of a state or condition. A state that is the ultimate state of human knowledge. When a man attains a rare state (bodhisattva) by his reason and knowledge, he is called 'Buddha'.

- Babasaheb Dr. Ambedkar has also been given the status of Bodhisattva, the work that Tathagata Gautam Buddha did because of his knowledge, Dr. Ambedkar did the same work because of his knowledge. So he too became a 'Bodhisattva'.

- There is strictness of law in religions. Whereas you are completely free to believe or not to believe in Dhamma.

- Dhamma does not impose any law on you. Everything is fixed in religion. Eg: Whatever is written in religious texts is true. Its observance is necessary at any cost. Whereas Dhamma considers change for the benefit of human beings depending on the circumstances. It has a scientific approach.

- Dhamma is 'knowledge'. That's why it can lead to an increase in argumentation and education. * * while religion is a man-made 'law'. Whatever these are blue and yellow, that is religion.

- Scientific reasoning is the basis of successful life.

Technology Of Anapana Meditation And Vipassana Technique With Mangal Maitri In Disciplined Ashram.

(Buddham Saranam Gacchami, Dhammam Saranam Gacchami, Sangham Saranam Gacchami)

As Per Gita Chapter-Vi Lord Krishna Told Arjuna To Perform Self Discipline Yog-This Yog explained that watch the front of Inhaling and Outhaling and watch and understand the sensation inside the body.

Lord Budha learn the technique and reached a stage of ULTIMATE Peace and teaches above technique around 45 years.The Technology is as under.-He has a Residential course of 48days and now it is of 10days, 15days, 20days, 30days, 60days and so.This is taught by their Assistant Teacher nowadays.

The Eightfold Path consists of eight practices: **right view, right resolve, right speech, right conduct, right livelihood, right effort, right mindfulness, and right samadhi** ('meditative absorption or union').

Division	Eightfold Path factors
Moral virtue (Sanskrit: *śīla*, Pāli: *sīla*)	1. Right speech
	2. Right action
	3. Right livelihood
Meditation (Sanskrit and Pāli: *samādhi*)	4. Right effort
	5. Right mindfulness
	6. Right concentration
Insight,wisdom (Sanskrit: *prajñā*, Pāli: *paññā*)	7. Right resolve
	8. Right view

Ashram discipline is compulsory and starts from 4am to night 9.30pm.

A.   DAILY ROUTINE-

4am- Wake Up Period

4.30am to 6.30am-Anapana Meditation/ Vipassana Technique Time

6.30am to 7.00am- Satvik Breakfast with 1 fruit

7am to 8am -Rest

8am to 11am-Anapana Meditation/ Vipassana Technique Time

11am to 11.30am-Satvik Lunch

11.30am to 1pm-Rest

1.00pm to 4.30pm- Anapana Meditation/ Vipassana Technique

4.30PM to 5.00PM- Tea/Ginger Soup/Lemon Juice Break.

5.00PM to 6.00PM -Rest

6PM to 9PM-Anapana Meditation/Vipassana Technique

9PM to 4AM- Rest

B.   Follow the Panchsheel Discipline.

1. **ANAPANA MEDITATION-** Just watch the incoming normal breath and outgoing normal breath.Technique is very simple,but tough to control,because mind is not staying a point for more than 10 second to 1 minute.Once it reaches to 1minute to 10 minute means life will get the direct energy from Nature.

- Practically it is difficult to make concentration on Breath,hence Lord Budha suggested an idea of Bhaw,there are three Bhaw of our vision either in closed eye or in open eye that is a. Bhokta Bhaw,b. Drasta Bhaw and c.Sleeping Bhaw. and other Bhaw is called Samta Bhaw.

- If we are keeping vision in Drasta Bhaw,our sight or concentration automatically reaches the nasal starting point where we can watch the Incoming and Outgoing breath easily and we can maintain it easily for 1 minute to 10 minute.

- Be like an Umbrella,Umbrella helping us from rain in Rainy Season and sun-ray in Summer Season.

- This is the technique to follow for 3 consecutive days to control mind on Inhaling and Outhaling.

- Day-0-Giving words to Teacher to Learn the Anapana Meditation Introduction and Introductory Classes.Understanding the Drasta Bhav and Bhokta Bhav and learning to concentrate on Nasal starting place.

- Day-1 Practice to keep concentration in front of Nasal point.Lesson to Learn the technique to watch the Inhaling inside the Nasal.

- Day-2 Practice to keep concentration of Inhaling inside the Nasal.Lesson to learn the Inhaling at Entry Point.

- Day-3to5 Practice Whole day and Evening Giving words to Learn Vipassana from Teacher and taking lesson to watch the different parts of body and feeling sensation.

2.   VIPASSANA TECHNIQUE-

The 15th day session is the complete teaching,while initially the 10 day session is sufficient,after experience join the 15th day,20 day,30day,60day session.This   cures the human body and human becoming like Children.Children is the real GOD. Watching the Sensation at every part of our body and feeling the sensation for 7 day.In 7th,8th,9th,10th,11th,12th,and 13th days the human body becomes fluid like volatile and energy movement becomes very fast.It cures from ill health trouble.Details is as under.

- Day-3 Practice Whole day and Evening Giving words to Learn Vipassana from Teacher and taking lessons to watch the different parts of body and feeling sensation,Or practice the Anapana Meditation.

- Day-4,Watching Each part of the body for 1 minute and feeling happiness.Taking Lessons to concentrate on Sensible and Insensible parts of the Body,Or practice the Anapana Meditation.

- Day-5,Concentration on the Insensible part of the body more and understanding the Sense and no reply for any sense.Learn the technique to Concentrate to Parallel Organ like both side hand etc,Or practice the Anapana Meditation and Evening Giving words to Learn Vipassana from Teacher.

- Day-6,Concentrate to parallel Organ.Learn the technique to Concentrate from top to Bottom and Bottom to Top.

- Day-7,Concentrate from Top to Bottom and Bottom to Top.Learn the technique of Feeling of Flow of Energy from Top to Bottom and Bottom to Top.

- Day-8 Practice to Flow of Energy from Top to Bottom and Bottom to Top.Learn the Technique of Bhang Yog.

- Day-9,Practice to Bhang Yog, that is free flow from Top to Bottom and Bottom to Top.Learn the technique to understand the Vedna of Inhaling and Outhaling in different parts of Body with Bhang Yog.
- 10th day focussing on Vedana means inhaling and feeling air entering and outing to other parts of the body.Learn the Technique of sensation in Kaya means in the skeleton of human body with Bhang yog.
- 11th day focusing on Kaya means the whole skeleton and we are feeling the sensation in bone and inside of bones.Learn the technique of understanding of Chit sensation with Bhang Yog.
- 12th day focussing in Chit means whole chit and we are feeling the sensation in chit.Learning the technique to understand Sensation of Dharma and controlling of Dharma with Bhang Yog.
- 13th day focussing on Dharma and we are feeling the sensation of Dharma for the world with Bhang Yog.Learning the technique to understand the Mangal Maity Session.

3.   MANGAL MAITRI

- 14th day is for Mangal Maitri day.and returning to the routine Life
- 15th day-End session after morning session.

This Technique Also Called **Mantra Tantra And Yantra Sadhna.**

- **Mantra is watching the Respiration,Tantra is feeling sensation in Body and Yantra is feeling sensation in inside Organ.**
- **It cures the whole body and human beings become like a Children.**
- **This cures our six senses Brain,Ear,Skin,Eye,Teeth,and Nose corresponding to Nature,Sound,Touchment or Attachment, facial,taste and smell.**

- Increasing the Mangal Maitri from 5 minute to 24x7 hours brings practitioners from ARIHANT Position to IMMORTAL Position.

Jainism

BASICS-

JAIN Strictly practicing the Chapter-3,6,7,8,12,13.14.15.16.17 & 18 ,JAIN also has its own Strict Way of Life.His Chanting mantra is Jai Jinendra and **NAVKAR MANTRA IS-**

Ṇamō Arihantāṇaṁ,Ṇamō Siddhāṇaṁ,Ṇamō Ayariyāṇaṁ,Ṇamō Uvajjhāyāṇaṁ,Ṇamō Lōē Savva Sāhūṇaṁ,Ēsōpancaṇamōkkārō, savvapāvappaṇāsaṇō,Maṅgalā ṇaṁ ca savvēsiṁ, paḍamama havaī maṅgalaṁ.

|| णमोकार मंत्र ||
णमो अरिहंताणं,
णमो सिद्धाणं,
णमो आयरियाणं,
णमो उवज्झायाणं,
णमो लोए सव्व साहुणं,
एसो पंच णमोक्कारो, सव्व पावप्पणसणो ।
मंगलाणं च सव्वेसिं, पढमं हवइ मंगलं ||

Main teaching is to follow the Ayurvedic lifestyle, Non-violence,Ahimsa,Aparigraha and Moksha is achieved to follow Astangik marg, perform Meditation Sāmāyika which is done for 48 mins in peace and silence.

INTRODUCTION-

The meaning of 'Jainism' is - 'the religion promoted by Jin'.

Jainism was founded by Rishabhdev who was born in Ayodhya and his symbol was bull.

According to Jain texts, Mahavir or Vardhaman attained Nirvana 527 years before Christ. Jainism is one of the oldest religions in the world, originating in India at least 2,500 years ago. The spiritual goal of Jainism is to break free from the endless cycle of rebirth and attain an omniscient state called moksha. The founder of Jainism is considered to be Rishabh Dev, who was the first Tirthankara of Jainism and father of Bharata, the Chakravarti emperor of India. Jinendra is used for souls who have lost their minds. have conquered the word and the body and have attained only knowledge. On the return of Bhadrabahu, he had a deep disagreement with the sages of Magadha, as a result of which Jainism split into two sects called Svetambara and Digambara. The disciples of Sthulabhadra were called Shvetambaras (wearing white robes) and the disciples of Bhadrabahu were called Digambaras (those who were naked).

(a) In the Digambara sect, nudity is said to be the main for salvation, while the Shvetambaras do not consider nudity to be necessary to attain salvation.

(b) The Digambaras forbid women's emancipation, the 19th Tirthankara Mallinath is accepted as Mallikumari in the Shvetambara tradition. Sammed Shikhar, Rajgir, Pavapuri, Girnar, Shatrunjay, Shravanabelagola etc. are famous pilgrimages of Jains.

The earth is naked, so the Digambaras are naked.

The life of a sage is spotless, so no clothes are needed to hide it.

Clothes are needed by those who have to hide something.

The basic reason behind not wearing clothes was also told that wearing clothes would hinder their sadhana.

The holy book is known as Agam Sahitya or Agam Sutra.

Even the few preachers who survived, many evils came.

Eight Arya Marg

Right vision, Right will,Right speech, Right action, Right livelihood, Right exercise, Right memory and Right meditation.

According to the Jain texts (Agam), the present-day Jainism came into vogue from the time of Lord Adinath.

The Tirthankara tradition that started from here continued till Lord Mahavira or Vardhamana who attained Nirvana 527 years before Christ.

This concert took place during the reign of Maurya ruler Chandragupta Maurya.

The first Jain monk was Champa, the daughter of King Dadhivahana.

During his lifetime, Mahavira founded a sangha in which 11 prominent followers were involved.

According to tradition, Lord Rishabhdev became the first Tirthankar during this period, followed by the 23rd Tirthankara Bhagwan Parshvanath (877-777 BCE) and the 24th Tirthankara Mahavir Swami (599-527 BCE)/(618-546BCE).

According to the Shvetambara sect, 609 years after Mahavira Nirvana (83 AD) in Rathavipur, the Botic school (Digambar) was founded by Shivbhuti.

TEACHINGS-

Jainism teaches that every living being is responsible for his own actions.

In Jainism, the sages easily tolerate the most difficult austerities, remain naked, whatever the weather, they walk in the footsteps, no matter how long the journey may be.

Once they take food, that too while standing.

One of these basic qualities is hard penance, Keshaloncha

The subtle trasas and immovable creatures in the cracks of the land, while bathing, suffer from the water of the bath, that is why Jain monks do not take baths.

Bathing with violence is also said to be taboo for being the cause of Vibhusha.

If we eat food while standing, then it is eaten with a full stomach. If they eat with a full stomach, then laziness will come and they will not be able to do sadhna. It is a belief that if there is no strength to stand, then the time has come to take samadhi.

Non-violence is the basic principle of Jainism. It is followed very strictly, it can be seen especially in the rules of eating conduct.

In Jain philosophy, every particle is independent, there is no doer of this creation or any living being.

All living beings enjoy the fruits of their own actions.

The teachings of Jainism emphasize the ideas of equality, non-violence, spiritual liberation and self-control. What Mahavir has taught to the ages is still important in modern life. Jains are an important religious community and Jainism preaches on various principles of virtue that enrich the population.

SAMAYIKA MEDITATION

Jain meditation is also referred as Sāmāyika which is done for 48 mins in peace and silence.

A form of this which includes a strong component of scripture study (Svādhyāya) is mainly promoted by the Digambara tradition of Jainism.

The word Sāmāyika means being in the moment of continuous real-time. The best technique in Jainism is to feel our breathing through inhaling and exhaling. It can be felt at the top of the nose and deep inside the nose.

Meditation can be broadly classified as - Shubh (Dharma Dhyana and Shukla Dhyana) and Inauspicious (Arta Dhyana and Rudra Dhyana).

1. *Arta-Dhyana,* "a mental condition of suffering, agony and anguish." Usually caused by thinking about an object of desire or a painful ailment.

2. *Raudra-Dhyana,* associated with cruelty, aggressive and possessive urges.

3. *Dharma-Dhyana,* "virtuous" or "customary", refers to knowledge of the soul, the non-soul and the universe. Over time this became associated with discriminating knowledge (*bheda-vijñāna*) of the tattvas (truths or fundamental principles).

4. *Sukla-Dhyana* (pure or white), divided into (1) Multiple contemplation, (*pṛthaktva-vitarka-savicāra*); (2) Unitary contemplation, (*aikatva-vitarka-nirvicāra*); (3) Subtle infallible physical activity (*sūkṣma-kriyā-pratipāti*); and (4) Irreversible stillness of the soul (*vyuparata-kriyā-anivarti*). The first two are said to require knowledge of the lost Jain scriptures known as purvas and thus it is considered by some Jains that pure meditation was no longer possible. The other two forms are said in the Tattvartha sutra to be only accessible to Kevalins (enlightened ones).[38

Sikhism

BASIC-

SIKHISM Strictly followed the Chapter-3,5,6,12 & 18. KHALSA have their own strict Way of Life. Mantra is-Waheguru ii ka Khalsa, sri Waheguru ji ki fateh. There are three core tenets of the Sikh religion: Meditation upon and devotion to the Creator, truthful living, and service to humanity. Naam Japna is meditation on God through reciting, chanting, singing and concentration on Him.

Sikhism developed from the spiritual teachings of Guru Nanak (1469–1539), the faith's first guru, and the nine Sikh gurus who succeeded him.

The tenth guru, Gobind Singh (1666–1708), named the Sikh scripture *Guru Granth Sahib* as his successor, bringing to a close the line of human gurus and establishing the scripture as the 11th and last eternally living guru, a religious spiritual/life guide for Sikhs.

Guru Nanak taught that living an "active, creative, and practical life" of "truthfulness, fidelity, self-control and purity" is above metaphysical truth, and that the ideal man "establishes union with God, knows His Will, and carries out that Will".

Guru Hargobind, the sixth Sikh Guru (1606–1644), established the concept of mutual co-existence of the *miri* ('political'/'temporal') and *piri* ('spiritual') realms. The Sikh scripture opens with the *Mul Mantar* (□□□ □□□□), fundamental prayer about *ik onkar* (□, 'One God').

The core beliefs of Sikhism, articulated in the *Guru Granth Sahib*, include faith and meditation in the name of the one creator; divine unity and equality of all humankind; engaging in *seva* ('selfless service'); striving for justice for the benefit and prosperity of all; and honest conduct and livelihood while living a householder's life. Following this standard, Sikhism rejects claims that any particular religious tradition has a monopoly on Absolute Truth. Sikhism emphasizes *simran* (□□□□□, meditation and remembrance of the teachings of Gurus), which can be expressed musically through *kirtan*, or internally through *naam japna* ('meditation on His name') as a means to feel God's presence.

It teaches followers to transform the "Five Thieves" (i.e. lust, rage(Uncontrolled anger), greed, attachment, and ego).

Service and Action

The Sikh gurus taught that by constantly remembering the divine name (*naam simran*) and through selfless service (*sēvā*) the devotee overcomes egotism (*Haumai*). This, it states, is the primary root of five evil impulses and the cycle of birth and death.

Service in Sikhism takes three forms:

TAN,MAN AND DHAN *Tan* (physical service, i.e. labor), *Man* (mental service, such as dedicating your heart for service of others), and *Dhan* (material service, including financial support). Sikhism stresses *kirat karō*: that is "honest work". Sikh teachings also stress the concept of sharing, or *vaṇḍ chakkō*, giving to the needy for the benefit of the community. The gurdwara is also the location for the historic Sikh practice of "Langar" or the community meal. All gurdwaras are open to anyone of any faith for a free meal, always vegetarian. People eat together, and the kitchen is maintained and serviced by Sikh community volunteers.

Initiation and the Khalsa

Khalsa (meaning "pure and sovereign") is the collective name given by Guru Gobind Singh to those Sikhs who have been fully initiated by taking part in a ceremony called *amrit sañcār* (nectar ceremony).

The first time that this ceremony took place was on Vaisakhi, which fell on 30 March 1699 at Anandpur Sahib in Punjab.It was on that occasion that Gobind Singh baptized the **Pañj Piārē** – the five beloved ones, who in turn baptized Guru Gobind Singh himself. To males who initiated, the last name Singh, meaning "lion", was given, while the last name Kaur, meaning "princess", was given to baptized Sikh females.

Baptized Sikhs wear five items, called the Five Ks (in Punjabi known as *pañj kakkē* or *pañj kakār*), at all times. The five items are: *kēs* (uncut hair), *kaṅghā* (small wooden comb), *kaṛā* (circular steel or iron bracelet), *kirpān* (sword/dagger), and *kacchera* (special undergarment).The Five Ks have both practical and symbolic purposes.

Upon a child's birth, the Guru Granth Sahib is opened at a random point and the child is named using the first letter on the top left hand corner of the left page. All boys are given the last name Singh, and all girls are given the last name Kaur (this was once a title which was conferred on an individual upon joining the Khalsa).

The Sikh marriage ritual includes the *anand kāraj* ceremony. The marriage ceremony is performed in front of the Guru Granth Sahib by a baptized Khalsa, Granthi of the Gurdwara.The tradition of circling the Guru Granth Sahib and Anand Karaj among Khalsa is practiced since the fourth Guru, Guru Ram Das. Its official recognition and adoption came in 1909, during the Singh Sabha Movement. Upon death, the body of a Sikh is usually cremated. If this is not possible, any respectful means of disposing of the body may be employed. The *kīrtan sōhilā* and *ardās* prayers are performed during the funeral ceremony (known as *antim sanskār*).

Zoroastrian

ZOROASTRIAN follow Chapter-3,12,13,14,15,16,17 & 18 and have their own Way of Life. Mantra-Ashem Vohu ("**Truth is best (of all that is) good. As desired, as desired, truth.**")

The motto of Zoroastrianism is "**Good thoughts, good words, good deeds**"

BASIC-

Zoroastrians believe that there is one universal, transcendent, all-good, and uncreated supreme creator deity, Ahura Mazda, or the "Wise Lord" (*Ahura* meaning "Lord" and *Mazda* meaning "Wisdom" in Avestan).

Zoroaster keeps the two attributes separate as two different concepts in most of the Gathas yet sometimes combines them into one form. Zoroaster also claims that Ahura Mazda is omniscient but not omnipotent.

In the Gathas, Ahura Mazda is noted as working through emanations known as the Amesha Spent and with the help of "other ahuras",of which Sraosha is the only one explicitly named of the latter category. Scholars and theologians have long debated on the nature of Zoroastrianism, with dualism, monotheism, and polytheism being the main terms applied to the religion. Some scholars assert that Zoroastrianism's concept of divinity covers both being and mind as immanent entities, describing Zoroastrianism as having a belief in an immanent self-creating universe with consciousness as its special attribute, thereby putting Zoroastrianism in the pantheistic fold sharing its origin with Indian Hinduism.

In any case, Asha, the main spiritual force which comes from Ahura Mazda,is the cosmic order which is the antithesis of chaos, which is evident as *druj*, falsehood and disorder.

The resulting cosmic conflict involves all of creation, mental/spiritual and material, including humanity at its core, which has an active role to play in the conflict.

PRACTICALITY-

Zoroastrian theology includes foremost the importance of following the Threefold Path of Asha revolving around Good Thoughts, Good Words, and Good Deeds. There is also a heavy emphasis on spreading happiness, mostly through charity, and respecting the spiritual equality and duty of both men and women. Zoroastrianism's emphasis on the protection and veneration of nature and its elements has led some to proclaim it as the "world's first proponent of ecology. "The Avesta and other texts call for the protection of water, earth, fire and air making it, in effect, an ecological religion: "It is not surprising that Mazdaism…is called the first ecological religion. The reverence for Yazatas (divine spirits) emphasizes the preservation of nature. However, this particular assertion is limited to natural forces held as emanations of asha by the fact that early Zoroastrians had a duty to exterminate "evil" species, a dictate no longer followed in modern Zoroastrianism.

Zoroastrianism is not entirely uniform in theological and philosophical thought, especially with historical and modern influences having a significant impact on individual and local beliefs, practices, values and vocabulary, sometimes merging with tradition and in other cases displacing it. The ultimate purpose in the life of a practicing Zoroastrian is to become an *ashavan* (a master of Asha) and to bring happiness into the world, which contributes to the cosmic battle against evil.

The core teachings of Zoroastrianism include:
- Following the threefold path of Asha: *Humata, Hūxta, Huvarshta* ('good thoughts, good words, good deeds').

- Practicing charity to keep one's soul aligned with Asha and thus with spreading happiness.
- The spiritual equality and duty of men and women alike.
- Being good for the sake of goodness and without the hope of reward .

Practices

The religion states that active and ethical participation in life through good deeds formed from good thoughts and good words is necessary to ensure happiness and to keep chaos at bay. This active participation is a central element in Zoroaster's concept of free will and Zoroastrianism as such rejects extreme forms of asceticism and monasticism but historically has allowed for moderate expressions of these concepts.

In Zoroastrian tradition, life is a temporary state in which a mortal is expected to actively participate in the continuing battle between Asha and Druj. Prior to its incarnation at the birth of the child, the *urvan* (soul) of an individual is still united with its *fravashi* (personal/higher spirit), which has existed since Ahura Mazda created the universe. Prior to the splitting off of the *urvan* the fravashi participates in the maintenance of creation led by Ahura Mazda. During the life of a given individual, the fravashi acts as a source of inspiration to perform good actions and as a spiritual protector.

The fravashis of ancestors cultural, spiritual, and heroic, associated with illustrious bloodlines, are venerated and can be called upon to aid the living. On the fourth day after death, the urvan is reunited with its fravashi, whereupon the experiences of life in the material world are collected for use in the continuing battle for good in the spiritual world. For the most part, Zoroastrianism does not have a notion of reincarnation. Followers of Ilm-e-Khshnoom in India believe in reincarnation and practice vegetarianism, among other currently non-traditional opinions, although there have been various theological statements supporting vegetarianism in Zoroastrianism's history and claims that Zoroaster was vegetarian. In Zoroastrianism, water (*aban*) and fire (*atar*) are agents of ritual purity, and the associated purification ceremonies are considered the basis of ritual life. In Zoroastrian cosmogony, water and fire are respectively the second and last primordial elements to have been created, and scripture considers fire to have its origin in the waters (re. which conception see Apam Napat). Both water and fire are considered life-sustaining, and both water and fire are represented within the precinct of a fire temple. Zoroastrians usually pray in the presence of some form of fire (which can be considered evident in any source of light), and the culminating rite of the principal act of worship constitutes a "strengthening of the waters".

Fire is considered a medium through which spiritual insight and wisdom are gained, and water is considered the source of that wisdom.

Both fire and water are also hypothesized as the Yazatas Atar and Anahita, which worship hymns and litanies dedicated to them.

Ritual and prayer -

The central ritual of Zoroastrianism is the Yasna, which is a recitation of the eponymous book of the Avesta and sacrificial ritual ceremony involving Haoma. Extensions to the Yasna ritual are possible through use of the Visperad and Vendidad, but such an extended ritual is rare in modern Zoroastrianism. The Yasna itself descended from Indo-Iranian sacrificial ceremonies and animal sacrifice of varying degrees are mentioned in the Avesta and are still practiced in Zoroastrianism albeit through reduced forms such as the sacrifice of fat before meals. High rituals such as the Yasna are considered to be the purview of the Mobeds with a corpus of individual and communal rituals and prayers included in the Khordeh Avesta.

A Zoroastrian is welcomed into the faith through the Navjote/Sedreh Pushi ceremony, which is traditionally conducted during the later childhood or pre-teen years of the aspirant, though there is no defined age limit for the ritual. After the ceremony, Zoroastrians are encouraged to wear their sedreh (ritual shirt) and kusti (ritual girdle) daily as a spiritual reminder and for mystical protection, though reformist Zoroastrians tend to only wear them during festivals, ceremonies, and prayers. The incorporation of cultural and local rituals is quite common and traditions have been passed down in historically Zoroastrian communities such as herbal healing practices, wedding ceremonies, and the like.

Traditionally, Zoroastrian rituals have also included shamanic elements involving mystical methods such as spirit travel to the invisible realm and involving the consumption of fortified wine, Haoma, mang, and other ritual aids.

Historically, Zoroastrians are encouraged to pray the five daily Gāhs and to maintain and celebrate the various holy festivals of the Zoroastrian calendar, which can differ from community to community. Zoroastrian prayers, called mantras, are conducted usually with hands outstretched in imitation of Zoroaster's prayer style described in the Gathas and are of a reflectionary and supplicant nature believed to be endowed with the ability to banish evil.Devout Zoroastrians are known to cover their heads during prayer, either with traditional topi, scarves, other headwear, or even just their hands. However, full coverage and veiling which is traditional in Islamic practice is not a part of Zoroastrianism and Zoroastrian women in Iran wear their head coverings displaying hair and their faces to defy mandates by the Islamic Republic of Iran.

Ajivika

(A Way Of Life)

BASICS-

Followed the GITA Chapter-3,4,5,12,13,14,15,16,&17 and have their own way of Life. Makhali Ghoshal is the founder of Ajivika Movement. Main Idea is that whatever is happening in the world is NIYTI (Law of Nature). Humans have to Work without attachment, Lust and Greed.

CONCEPT-

The name *Ajivika* for an entire philosophy resonates with its core belief in "no free will" and complete *niyati*, literally "inner order of things, self-command, pre-determinism", leading to the premise that good simple living is not a means to salvation or moksha, just a means to true livelihood, predetermined profession and way of life.

The name came to imply that school of Indian philosophy which lived a good simple mendicant-like livelihood for its own sake and as part of its predeterministic beliefs, rather than for the sake of after-life or motivated by any soteriological(Salvation)reasons. According to ancient Tamil Literature the concept was known as "Aaseevagam" Which when splitted gives three words "Aasu" (ஆசு) means perfect + "eevu"(ஈவு) means solution + "Agham"(அகம்) means resides. Which gives a meaning to the path which contains the perfect solution for life. The concepts of Aaseevaham are pretty scattered in the Tamil epics of "Silappadikaram" and "Kundalakesi". The Concepts followed by Aasevagam are still followed in many villages of Tamil Nadu. It is believed the famous temple of Sabaramalai is built in the principle of Aaseevaham.

Ājīvika philosophy is cited in ancient texts of Buddhism and Jainism to Makkhali Gosala, a contemporary of the Buddha and Mahavira. In *Sandaka Sutta* the Ājīvikas are said to recognize three emancipators: Nanda Vaccha, Kisa Sankicca, and Makkhali Gosāla. Exact origins of Ājīvika is unknown, but generally accepted to be the 5th century BCE.

The Ājīvika philosophy spread rapidly in ancient South Asia, with a *Sangha Geham* (community center) for Ājīvikas on the island now known as Sri Lanka and also extending into the western state of Gujarat by the 4th century BCE, the era of the Maurya Empire

Evidence suggests that emperor Ashoka, in the 3rd century BCE, considered Ājīvikas to be more closely related to the schools of Hinduism than to Buddhists, Jainas or other Indian schools of thought.

The problems of time and change was one of the main interests of the Ajivikas. Their views on this subject may have been influenced by Vedic sources, such as the hymn to *Kala* (Time) in Atharvaveda. Both Jaina and Buddhist texts state that Ājīvikas believed in absolute determinism, absence of free will, and called this *niyati*. Everything in human life and universe, according to Ajivikas, was predetermined, operating out of cosmic principles, and true choice did not exist. The Buddhist and Jaina sources describe them as strict fatalists, who did not believe in karma.

The Ajivikas philosophy held that all things are preordained, and therefore religious or ethical practice has no effect on one's future, and people do things because cosmic principles make them do so, and all that will happen or will exist in future is already predetermined to be that way.

No human effort could change this *niyati* and the karma ethical theory was a fallacy. James Lochtefeld summarizes this aspect of Ajivika belief as, "life and the universe is like a ball of pre-wrapped up string, which unrolls until it is done and then goes no further".

Riepe states that the Ajivikas belief in predeterminism does not mean that they were pessimistic. Rather, just like Calvinists belief in predeterminism in Europe, the Ajivikas were optimists. The Ajivikas simply did not believe in the moral force of action, or in merits or demerits, or in after-life to be affected because of what one does or does not do. Actions had immediate effects in one's current life but without any moral traces, and both the action and the effect was predetermined, according to the Ajivikas. Makkhali Gosala seems to have combined the ideas of older schools of thought into an eclectic doctrine.

He appears to have believed in *niyati* (destiny), *svabhava* (nature), and *sangati* (change), and possibly *parinama*, which may have prompted other philosophical schools to label him variously as *ahetuvadin*, *vainayikavadin*, *ajnanavadin*, and *issarakaranavadin*. According to him all beings undergo development (*parinama*). This culminates in the course of time (*samsarasuddhi*) in final salvation to which all beings are destined under the impact of the factors of *niyati* (destiny), *bhava* (nature), and *sangati* (change). As such destiny does not appear as the only player, but rather chance or indeterminism plays equal part in his doctrine. He thus subscribed to *niyativada* (fatalism) only in the sense that he thought that *some* future events like salvation for all were strictly determined.

Ajivika was an atheistic philosopher. They did not presume any deity as the creator of the universe, or as prime mover, or that some unseen mystical end was the final resting place of the cosmos.

In later texts, the Tamil *Nīlakēci*, a story of two divinities, Okkali and Ōkali, relates the Ājīvikas instructed men in the scriptures.

Ajivikas believed that in every being there is a soul (Atman). However, unlike Jains and various orthodox schools of Hinduism that held that the soul is formless, Ajivikas asserted that the soul has a material form, one that helps meditation. They also believed that the soul passes through many births and ultimately progresses unto its pre-destined *nirvana* (salvation).Basham states that some texts suggest evidence of Vaishnavism-type devotional practices among some Ajivikas.

Atomism

Ajivikas developed a theory of elements and atoms similar to the Vaisheshika school of Hinduism. Everything was composed of minuscule atoms, according to Ajivikas, and qualities of things are derived from aggregates of atoms, but the aggregation and nature of these atoms was predetermined by cosmic forces.

The description of Ajivikas atomism is inconsistent between those described in Buddhist and Hindu texts. According to three Tamil texts,the Ajivikas held there exists seven *kayas* (Sanskrit: काय, assemblage, collection, elemental categories): *pruthvi-kaya* (earth), *apo-kaya* (water), *tejo-kaya* (fire), *vayo-kaya* (air), *sukha* (joy), *dukkha* (sorrow) and *jiva* (life). The first four relate to matter, the last three non-matter.

These elements are *akata* (that which is neither created nor destroyed), *vanjha* (barren, that which never multiplies or reproduces) and have an existence independent of the other.The elements, asserts Ajivika theory in the Tamil text Manimekalai, are made of *paramanu* (atoms), where atoms were defined as that which cannot be further subdivided, that which cannot penetrate another atom, that which is neither created nor destroyed, that which retains its identity by never growing or expanding nor splitting nor changing, yet that which moves, assembles and combines to form the perceived. The Tamil text of Ajivikas asserts that this "coming together of atoms can take a diversity of forms, such as the dense form of a diamond, or a loose form of a hollow bamboo". Everything one perceives, states the atomism theory of Ajivikas, was mere juxtapositions of atoms of various types, and the combinations occur always in fixed ratios governed by certain cosmic rules, forming *skandha* (molecules, building blocks). Atoms, asserted the Ajivikas, cannot be seen by themselves in their pure state, but only when they aggregate and form *bhutas* (objects). They further argued that properties and tendencies are characteristics of the objects. The Ajivikas then proceeded to justify their belief in determinism and "no free will" by stating that everything experienced – *sukha* (joy), *dukkha* (sorrow) and *jiva* (life) – is mere function of atoms operating under cosmic rules. Riepe states that the details of the Ajivikas theory of atomism provided the foundations of later modified atomism theories found in Jain, Buddhist and Hindu tradition

Every day we hear the laments of the older generations that the youth these days are not religious. They don't believe in God or in the teachings of Vedas. They continue to blame science and technology for the same. However, it is not true that atheism is a modern concept – rather it dates back to many millennia.

In 6th century BC, a religious movement started against Brahmanism, (the belief in God and the Vedas.) This led to the start of the Sramana Movement that is the creation of an atheist or nastika school of thought – this philosophy didn't accept the concept of deities, God, a higher power or Vedas. This school of thought was further classified into materialistic atheism and ethical atheism. In this article we will focus only on a single branch of ethical atheism, that is the Ajivika philosophy in India.

The major beliefs of the Ajivikas are as below

- **Soul** – The Ajivikas are different from other atheist schools of thought because while they discarded the concept of God or any other higher power, they retained the idea of 'Atma' or soul, which implied they believed in the life and death cycle. They didn't however believe in Moksha as a way of liberation but rather 'Bhagya' determined liberation from the burden of karma.

- **Atomism** – The concept of atoms in the ajivika philosophy is similar to the orthodox Nyaya-vaisheshika philosophy. According to this theory everything is made of atoms and the arrangement of atoms is determined by the physical laws of nature and thereby affecting its shape and being. The only difference between these two philosophies is that Ajivika school believed that the soul is also made up of atoms.

- **Fatalism (absolute determinism)** – From the earlier point we know that the soul is made up of atoms and since everything is arranged in a predetermined way by nature, it leads to the fact that even life is predetermined. This idea is called 'Niyati' , that is fate. While this idea of absolute determinism may help in dealing with the stresses in life it also shows us that there is no free will of the individual. And it is also this principle in philosophy that has been attacked by the other schools of thought. According to the texts, if the actions of an individual are predetermined and he has no control over them then he is not responsible for it either. Since one has no responsibility for his deeds whether good or bad, there is no motivation to be good either, thereby leading to lawlessness and disorder in society. It also attacks the very root of the concept of cause-effect relationship or 'karma-phala' (idea that we carry the fruits or punishments of our past lives into the next one. This cycle continues until the deeds and its consequences are balanced), which is fundamental to Hinduism.

It is mentioned in Sumanna-phala sutta that when the Buddha along with 1250 bhikkhus was stationed at Rajagriha, King Ajatashatru felt in need of spiritual 3 Section 12.6 and 12.7 have been written by Dr. Suchi Dayal 222 Vedic Period and Cultures in Transition guidance.

His ministers then suggested the names of the following heretical teachers one by one

1) Purana Kassapa

2) Makkali Gosala

3) Ajita Kesakambali

4) Pakudha Kaccayana

5) Sanjaya Belatthiputta

6) Nigantha Nataputta

Each is referred to as the leader of an order,well known, famous, the founder of a sect,respected as a saint (sadhu-sammato), revered by many people, a homeless wanderer of long standing and advanced in years.

Now let us discuss the teachings of each briefly:

1) Purana Kassapa preached the doctrine of Akriya or non-action. He was a brahmana teacher whose main doctrine was that action did not lead to either merit or demerit. According to him, even if a man killed all the creatures on earth, he would not incur any sin. Similarly, he would not earn any merit through good deeds or even by standing on the bank of Ganges. Similarly, self-control, gifts and truthfulness would not earn him any credit.

2) Makkhali Gosala: A doctrine of niyativada is prescribed. According to the most celebrated teacher of the Ajivika sect, Makkhali Gosala, there is no cause or basis for the sin of living beings. Neither is there cause or basis for the purity of living beings. No deed can affect one's future births. No human action, strength, courage and human endurance can affect one's destiny. All men are without power, strength or virtue. They are driven by destiny, chance and nature.

3) Ajita Kesakambali: There is no merit in alms-giving, sacrifice or offering. Good deeds or evil deeds do not lead to good karma or bad karma respectively.

There is no transmigration of souls. No ascetic can reach perfection on the right path. Man is formed of four elements: when he dies, earth returns to the aggregate of earth; water to water; fire to fire; air to air; while the sense vanishes into space.

4) Pakudha Kaccayana: There are seven immutable elements. These are: the bodies of earth, fire, water, air, joy, sorrow, life. Even if a man cuts off the head of another with a sword, he does not take life as his sword passes through these seven elements. This is the theory of Asasvatavada. These seven elements do not lead to any pleasure or pain.

5) Sanjaya Belatthiputta: If you asked me, "Is there another world?" and if I believed that there was, I should tell you so. But that is not what I say. I do not say that it is so; I do not say that it is otherwise; I do not say that it is not so; nor do I say that it is not not so. Clearly the above-mentioned lines underline the satirical nature; a tilt at agnostic teachers who are not willing to give any definite answer to any metaphysical question put to them.

6) Nigantha Nataputta: Nigantha can be identified with Vardhamana Mahavira, the 24th tirthankara of Jainism. According to the passage, the four-fold restraint is a barrier that surrounds a nigantha. By avoiding all sin, he becomes perfected, controlled and firm. Ajivikas The most prominent teacher of the Ajivika sect was Makkali Gosala.

Sanatan (Hinduism)

SANATAN have the option to follow all chapters from 1 to 18 from Birth to Death in different different stages.Sanatan people follow the 16 Sanskar,which comes in different phases of life which includes the 18 chapter of GITA.

There are Nine works divided which indicate to perform any work with devotion,that work will give peace to the concerned People.

Sacred Sixteen Sacraments of Hinduism (SANATAN)

Hinduism(Sanatan) is the main religio n of India. In this, sixteen sacred rites are performed. Due to the antiquity and vastness of Hinduism, it is also called 'Sanatan Dharma'. SANATAN(Hinduism), like Buddhism, Jainism, Christianity, Islam, etc., is not a Community established by any particular person, but a large set of different community and beliefs that have been going on since ancient times. According to Maharishi Ved Vyas, sixteen sacred sacraments are performed from birth to death.

Which is as follows :-

(1). Conception ceremony, (2). Punsavan rituals. (3). Seemantonnayan Sanskar, (4). Jatkarma Sanskar, (5). Naming Ceremony, (6). The evacuation ceremony, (7). Annaprashan Sanskar, (. Chudakarma Sanskar, (9). Vidyarambha Sanskar, (10. Karnavedha Sanskar, (11). Yagyopaveet Sanskar, (12). Vedarambh Sanskar, (13). Keshant Sanskar, (14). Samvartan Sanskar, (15). Marriage rites, (16). Funeral rites.

1. Garbhadhana-samskara (Conception): Maharishi Charak has said that it is necessary for pregnancy to be happy and strong in the mind, that is why men and women should always eat the answer food and remain happy always. At the time of conception, the mind of man and woman should be filled with enthusiasm, happiness and health.

In order to get a good child, first of all, conception-sanskar has to be done. Pregnancy is produced by the combination of Raj and Semen of the parents. This coincidence is called conception. The physical union of a man and a woman is called garbhadhana-samskara. After pregnancy, there are attacks of many types of natural defects, to avoid which this sanskar is performed.By which the pregnancy remains safe. Good and suitable progeny are produced from the insemination done with proper rituals.

2. Punsavan:: Punsavan Sanskar is organized after three months because the brain of the fetus starts developing after three months in the womb. At this time, the foundation of the sanskars of the child born in the womb is laid through the Punsavan Sanskar. According to the belief, the child starts learning in the womb, an example of this is Abhimanyu who had received the education of Chakravyuha in the womb of mother Subhdra.

3. Seemantonnayan- Seemantonnayan Sanskar is performed in the fourth, sixth and eighth months of pregnancy. At this time the child growing in the womb becomes capable of learning. To bring knowledge of good qualities, nature and deeds, the mother has to behave in the right way..During this, the mother should study by staying calm and happy.

4. Jatakram: By performing Jatkarma Sanskar as soon as the child is born, many types of defects of the child are removed.

Under this, on day six the baby is licked with honey and ghee, as well as Vedic mantras are recited so that the child is healthy and long.

On the basis of Jyotish Science Jatakarma is performed for a born child,this Sanskar helps families to train the Child in the same field for better development and benefit to the Society.

5. Naamkaran: After the Jatkarma, the naming ceremony is performed. On the basis of Jyotis , name suggests, the name of the child is kept in it. The naming ceremony is performed on the 11th day after the birth of the child. The name of the child is decided according to astrology. Many people name their child whatever is wrong. It affects his mindset and his future. Just as wearing good clothes enhances the personality, similarly having a good and concise name has its effect on the whole life. The thing to keep in mind is that the name of the child should be kept in such a way that he is called or known by that name at home and outside.

6. Nishkraman: After this, the Nishkraman ceremony is performed in the fourth month of birth. The meaning of expulsion is to take out.

Our body is made up of earth, water, fire, air and sky etc. which are called Panchabhutas. Therefore the father prays to these deities for the welfare of the child. Also wish the baby a long life and a healthy life.

7. Annaprashan: Annaprashan Sanskar is performed at the time of teething of the child i.e. at the age of 6-7 months. After this ritual, feeding of food to the child begins. In the beginning, well prepared food like kheer, khichdi, rice etc. is given.

8. Chudakarma: When the hair of the head is removed for the first time, then it is called Chudakarma or Mundan Sanskar.

When the child is one year old, or at the age of three, or at the age of the fifth or seventh year, the child's hair is plucked. This sanskar strengthens the child's head and sharpens the intellect. Along with this, the germs sticking in the hair of the baby are destroyed, due to which the baby gets health benefits.It is believed that after coming out of the womb, only the hair given by the parents remains on the head of the child.Cutting them leads to purification.

9. Karnavedha : The meaning of Karnavedh Sanskar is piercing the ear. There are five reasons for this, one- to wear jewelry. Second- Piercing the ear stops the bad effects of Rahu and Ketu according to astrology.

Third, it is acupuncture, due to which the flow of blood in the veins going to the brain starts to improve. Fourth, it increases hearing power and prevents many diseases. Fifth, it strengthens the sexual senses.

10. Yagyopavit: Yagyopavit is also called 5 to 48 days Upanayan or Janeu Sanskar.

Every Individual on the basis of their Birth caste performs this sanskar.

Brahmin,Kshtriya and Vaishya who are taking birth to work for society have a compulsory requirement to be the Dwij. The person who is taking birth in Shudra Caste,they are not required to be Dwij,because their birth quality is to Serve the Society in different ways.

Upa means to pass and Nayan means to carry.

To be taken to the Guru means to perform the Upanayana ceremony.

There are three,Six and Nine sutras in the Janeu i.e. Yagnopavit.

These are the symbols of three deities- Brahma, Vishnu, Mahesh.

This sanskar gives knowledge of Nature,strength, energy and radiance to the child. At the same time, a spiritual sense is awakened in him.

METHODOLOGY TO PERFORM UPNAYAN SANSKAR

Upnayan Sanskar is an old and Technical Sanskar which can change our Society in the Right Path. A few castes now follow this Sanskar and deliver it to the next Generation. #Guru, #Asst. Guru & #Sevak must be a SAINT and practical personal and away from all Greeds and who can devote 12 days and Night with Children and teach the Children from 4AM and their age should be 65+and Asst. Guru age be 50+. GURU must have 10 year experience as a Asst.Guru.Asst.Guru must have experience of min.10yrs as a SEVAK. SEVAK must be a person taken Upnayan Sanskar and following discipline from the last 10 years and without Greeds.Minimum age-21 years. Today we prepared a Guidelines in Stepwise such that we can improve the quality to our future generation, and present generation in Technical aspects such that our vision should run for a long time. Plan is for a minimum of 11 days with ARYA MOUN, which is essential for UPNAYAN SANSKAR.

DAY-1

Each PARENTS will make Puja of #KULDEVTA in Home and bring their son to Ashram till 2 PM with Light Clothes.

#Ashram will provide suitable Bed,Bed sheet and normal facility at ashram with suitable Chappal/Kharaw to all Children as guidelines of Guru & Asst. Guru.

5PM to 6PM -Dinner .

6PM-7.45PM- Introduction Classes by Guru & Asst. Guru. Delivery Speech for the programme of Upnayan Sanskar, Discipline of Ashram etc, start of #ARYA MOUN,and Dinner to Honorable Guest.

7.45PM-8.15PM-Day & Next day Programme discussion and Sense,Brain & Intellect Pranayam by GURU.

DAY-2

4AM-4.30AM- Wakeup and Become fresh with Bath.with help of Asst.Guru.

4.30AM-6.30AM-Guru Bandana+Sarvangasan Pranayama+Self Surrender Pranayama+LIFE ENERGY PRANAYAM+Sense Brain & Intellect Control Pranayam (Class-I)

6.30AM-7AM - Breakfast

7AM-11.00AM - Preparation by Children of Marwa+Matkor+Haldi Kalash in guideline of GURU.

11.00AM-11.45AM- Lunch

11.45AM to 1.30PM-Rest

1.30PM -3.30PM-Organising of Marwa+Matkor+Haldi kalash

3.30PM-5.30PM-Starting of Upnayan Sanskar+Ghrit Dhari+Puja of Satya Narayan Kath. Barua Dressing.

5.30PM-6.00PM-Dinner to Barua

6.00PM-7.45PM - Bhakti Yog by Barua with GURU+Dinner to Honorable Guest.

7.45PM -8.15PM - Day & Next day Programme discussion and Sense,Brain & Intellect Pranayam by GURU.

8.15PM-4AM - Rest.

DAY-3

4AM-4.30AM - Wakeup and Become fresh with Bath with help of Asst.Guru.

4.30AM-6.30AM-Guru Bandana+Sarvangasan Pranayama+Self Surrender Pranayama+LIFE ENERGY PRANAYAM+Sense Brain & Intellect Control Pranayam (Class-II)

6.30AM-7AM   - Breakfast

7AM-10.00AM - BHICHHATAN-I(External decided by Guru)

10.00AM-11.45AM- Preparation of Food & Lunch by Barua with GURU.

11.45AM to 1.30PM-Rest

1.30PM -3.00PM-Practice of Self Surrender & Life Energy Pranayama under Asst.Guru.3.00PM-4.30PM-Practice of Sense,Brain & Intellect Pranayama under Asst.Guru.

4.30PM-6.00PM-Preparation and Dinner to Barua under Guidance and with GURU.

6.00PM-7.45PM - Bhakti Yog by Barua under guidance of GURU+Dinner to Honorable Guest

7.45PM-8.15PM- Day & Next day Programme discussion and Self Control Pranayam by GURU.

8.15PM-4AM-REST

Day-4(Class-III) and BHICHHATAN-II(External decided by GURU),Rest similar as Day-3

Day-5(Class-IV),BICHHAWAN-III(External decided by GURU),Rest similar as Day-3

Day-6(Class-V),BHICHHATAN-IV(External decided by GURU),Rest similar as Day-3

Day-7(Class-VI),BHICHHATAN-V (External decided by GURU),Rest similar as Day-3

Day-8(Class-VII), BHICHHATAN-VI (External decided by GURU),Rest similar as Day-3

Day-9(Class-VIII), BHICHHATAN-VII (External decided byGURU),Rest similar as Day-3

Day-10(Class-IX), BHICHHATAN-VIII (External decided by GURU),Rest similar as Day-3

DAY-11

4AM-4.30AM - Wakeup and Become fresh with Bath with help of Asst. GURU.

4.30AM-6.30AM-SELF CONTROL MEDITATION(Class-X)

6.30AM-7AM   - Breakfast

7AM-10.00AM - BHICHHATAN-IX from own family

10.00AM-11.45AM- Preparation of Food & Lunch by Barua with GURU.

11.45AM to 1.30PM-Rest

1.30PM -4.30PM-Providing UPNAYAN

SANSKAR to all Barua.(END OF ARYA MOUN)

4.30PM-6.00PM-Preparation and Dinner by Barua under Guidance and with GURU.

6.00PM-7.45PM - Bhakti Yog by Barua under guidance of GURU+Dinner to Honorable Guest

7.45PM-8.15PM- Day & Next day Programme and Self Control Pranayam by GURU.

8.15PM-4AM-Rest.

DAY-12

4AM-4.30AM - Wakeup and Become fresh with Bath without help of Asst. GURU.

4.30AM-6.30AM-SELF CONTROL MEDITATION(Class-XI)

6.30AM-7AM   - Breakfast

7AM-9.00AM - Group Photographs and Discourse.

PARENTS WILL TAKE CARE OF CHILDREN.

END OF PROGRAMME

11.वेदारम्भ संस्कार

11. Vedarambh & Education: Under this the knowledge of Vedas is given to the person. After Veda knowledge people gets knowledge of their Birth Caste activity knowledge to strengthen the Economics of their family and Society

12. Samavartan: Samavartan Sanskar means to return again

After receiving education from the ashram or gurukul, this sanskar was performed to bring the person back into the society.

It means preparing a celibate person psychologically for the struggles of life.

13. Marriage & Economic Life: It is necessary to get married at an appropriate age. Marriage ceremony is considered to be the most important sacrament. Under this, both the bride and the groom stay together and get married, taking a vow to follow the right path. On the basis of Date of Birth,Place and Time the kundli Milan is the Ist step,after a matching marriage ceremony is held. Marriage does not only contribute to the development of the universe, but it is also necessary for the spiritual and mental development of a person. By this sanskar a person is also freed from the debt of the ancestors. Marriage is also strengthening their Economic Life.

14. Vanaprastha-It provides useful guidelines for peaceful departure from this world where the person comes for a limited period with a certain purpose.

ROUTINE-

1. Barefoot walking to a different TIRTH is the routine for this life.

2. Wake Up early in the morning at 4am.

3. Normally daily 12 KOS or 32 kilometer walking daily morning hour till 11am.

4. Eating twice Vegetarian food one before 12PM and 2nd before sunset.

5. Staying in a Temple or Ashram.

6. Performing morning puja and evening Meditation and some time talking with the public in afternoon time.

It is one's duty to pass on the mantle to the future generation without any attachment to one's own position.

It increases the Mangal Maitri.

15. SANYAS ASHRAM- In Hinduism(SANATAN) renunciation or sanyasa is the true mark of spiritual life.

It is believed to be the simple and straightforward way to achieve moksha or liberation.

Truly speaking, in the context of sanyasa or renunciation, the word, "achieve," is not the right word to use because "achieve" denotes materialism, seeking and striving for something, whereas in renunciation one has to give up worldly life and material possessions, and live without aiming for anything in particular, including the goal of salvation, liberation or union with God.

Having a purpose is important in worldly life, whereas not having any purpose is the central feature of renunciation or sannyasa in Hinduism.

A step which is the final path to increase the Mangal Maitri.His family is whole Nature.

TYPES OF SANYAS AND WORK-

Different types of Sanyas in the world are as under.

A. MONK B.Mandir Pujari C.Saint and performing Meditation in one place D.Saint and traveling to Tirth .D.Saint and performing meditation to construct the State or Country.E. Munni F. Father G. Saint and performing meditation and running school,Temple and Health Center.

16. Activity After Death or Funeral rites -

There is three activity after Death is as under-

1.When Arihant takes Samadhi,it is required to be put under the Earth or Water Samadhi or Well Samadhi or Forest Samadhi as desired by Arihant.

2.When a Child takes Death,it is required to be put under the Earth.

3. Normal people who get death due to poor health or by accident or else the dead body is offered to the Fire.

Thus sixteen sacraments are performed. ,

Antyashti Sanskar means funeral. After the death of a person i.e. renouncing the body, the dead body is offered to the fire.

Even today before the funeral procession, a fire is taken from the house by burning it.

DEVOTION- Bhakti is the foundation of all spiritual practice. It is both a means and an end in itself. What is the nature of Bhakti? The Narada Bhakti Sutras say: 'It is of the nature of supreme love towards **God**' (2nd Sutra).

Nine Ways of Devotion (Navadha Bhakti)

How does this love towards the divine manifest itself? The Srimad **Bhagavatam**,delineates the nine ways (Navadha Bhakti) in which we can lovingly connect with God:

1). Hearing about God (Shravana)

2). Chanting His Name and Glory (**Kirtana**)

3). Remembering Him (Smarana)

4). Serving His Lotus Feet (Pada Sevana)

5). Worshiping Him as per the Scriptures (Archana)

6). Prostrating before Him (Vandana)

7). Being His Servant (Dasya)

8). Befriending Him (Sakhya)

9). Offering Oneself to Him (Atma Nivedana)

1). Hearing about God (Shravana):

Listening to His divine name, His divine form, His Qualities, Actions, Mysteries etc., and getting lost in His glorious Lila is known as Shravana. Should we hear about God? Shri **Krishna** says in the **Gita**: "You can get that knowledge by humbly prostrating yourself before a Jnani Guru"

Mahamuni Shukadeva Narrating Bhagavata Purana to Raja Parikshata

Therefore, the first step in Shravana is to take recourse at the feet of a Guru. The Shravana aspect of Bhakti is exemplified most completely in King Parikshit, who listened to the Srimad Bhagavatam from the great sage Shukadeva. What effect did this listening have on Parikshit? At the end he said: "Respected Sukhdev Ji, you have made me experience the highest, fearless state. As a consequence I am now totally at peace. I am not afraid of death; let it come to me in any form now. I am totally fearless (Abhaya)" .

2). Chanting His Name and Glory (Kirtana):

Kirtana consists of chanting aloud God's divine name and glories of His form, His qualities, Mysteries, and Lilas; and, in the process of chanting, experiencing extreme thrill culminating in tears and a lightening of the heart.

Reconstructing Devotion Through Narada Bhakti Sutra

The very embodiment of Kirtana is the revered sage Narada. In fact, so engrossed is Narada in the act of Kirtana that he was actually happy when a curse was placed on him that he would not be able to stay in one place and would have to roam around the three worlds. Instead of lamenting this curse, he welcomed it saying that it would enable him to spread the Lord's name and glory all over the three worlds.

3). Remembering Him (Smarana):

Smarana means the constant remembrance of God. Krishna says in the Bhagavad Gita:

"The one who sees Me in everything and everything in Me, I am always present for him and he is always present for Me"

"Therefore, always keep Me in mind and then enter the battle of life. Undoubtedly you will attain unto me".

"The one who does not ruminate on anything else but constantly remembers me only, he finds it easy to reach Me".

As per the Srimad Bhagavatam:

"The mind which thinks of material objects becomes attached to those very objects. However, the mind which constantly remembers me, merges into Me"

Narasimha Drags Down The King Hiranyakashipu

An inspiring example of Smarana is Prahlada, who due to his constant remembrance of God was able to perceive Him everywhere. In fact, when his evil father ridiculed him saying that if God was everywhere, why did

He not show up in the pillar in front of them? The father then kicked the pillar, out of which sprang Lord Narasimha, validating the truth of Prahlada's conviction..

4). Serving His Lotus Feet (Pada Sevana):

The Srimad Bhagavatam says: 'Only till we have not taken recourse to the lotus feet of the Lord is there any cause of concern from money, family etc, which otherwise are a cause of fear and Dukha

Shesha Shayi Vishnu in Yoga Nidra

The obvious example of this kind of Bhakti is our mother **goddess Lakshmi**, who is seen in constant service of Lord **Vishnu's** lotus feet.

5). Worshiping Him as per the Scriptures (Archana):

Archana consists of the physical worship of God in the form of an idol etc, using the correct rituals (upacharas) as prescribed in the scriptures. These **rituals** consist of procedures like bathing and clothing the Deity, and also offering Him scents, **food** etc. An essential requirement of

Archana is the presence of faith (Shraddha) in the devotee. As Shri Krishna puts it in the Gita: "Whatever is offered to me, whether it be a leaf, flower, fruit or water, if it is done with Bhakti, I accept it".

Srimad Bhagavata: The Holy Book of God (Set of 4 Volumes)

An example of Archana Bhakti is that of King Prithu in the Srimad Bhagavatam, who satisfied Shri Vishnu with the selfless Vedic sacrifices he performed, so much so that the Lord presented Himself in person before the king.

6). Prostrating before Him (Vandana):

Vandana means prostrating oneself before the Lord. An illuminating example of this Bhakti is Akrura, another great personality in the Srimad Bhagavatam. The great Bhakta Akrura could not contain himself when he entered Vrindavana. He was overcome with emotion and the consequent surge of affection for Krishna made his hair stand on its end and the overflowing eyes began to shed tears. Akrura jumped onto the land of Vrindavana and rolled around on the earth saying: "Oh! This is the dust touched by the feet of my beloved Lord".

On going further, he saw Krishna milking the cows. The physical beauty of the Lord overwhelmed Akrura so much that he rushed down and prostrated himself at the feet of Krishna. Understanding Akrura's mental state, Krishna helped him to his feet, drew him to His heart and then embraced His beloved devotee".

7). Being His Servant (Dasya):

Being in selfless service of God, fulfilling His intentions and unquestioningly obeying all His orders is known as Dasya. The most powerful embodiment of this kind of Bhakti is undoubtedly Shri **Hanuman**, who as soon as he caught a glimpse of Shri **Rama**, declared himself to be the latter's servant.

Sri Rama Bhakta Hanuman Ji

Being a servant of God means leaving aside one's most important work to respectfully do the Lord's bidding; leaving all of one's own desires to fulfill His desire; considering even the greatest effort done for Him to be miniscule; thinking His ownership over our body to be greater than even our own; understanding that our wealth, life, body etc is useful only as long as it is in the use of God and so on. Hanuman had all these qualities, and no wonder that Shri Rama embraced him saying: "You are more dear to me than even Lakshmana" (**Ramayana of Tulsidas**).

8). Befriending Him (Sakhya):

Sakhya means personal friendship with God, a friendship in which there is a constant desire to stay in His company, and one enjoys conversations only with Him, and becomes extremely pleased on the mere mention of one's friend from a third person. Krishna Himself tells us who His friend is: "O Arjuna, you are both my friend and Bhakta".

The Mahabharata

Stories about the friendship of Krishna and Arjuna abound in the **Mahabharata** and Bhagavatam. Narratives show how they indulged in light banter, sports etc, which provide us with ample glimpses into the nature of their mutual friendship.

9). Offering Oneself to Him (Atma Nivedana):

Offering oneself wholly, including all of one's material possessions, with firm conviction, is known as Atmanivedana. The example of such surrender is king Bali, who was asked by an adolescent Brahmin for a piece of land equivalent to the distance measured by the latter's three footsteps. The Brahmin, who was none other than the Vamana Avatara of Lord Vishnu, measured out all the worlds with only two of His steps and finally there remained nowhere to place the promised third.

Vamana Purana with Hindi Translation

Seeing that there was no place left for Vamana's last step, Bali, bowing before Him, requested Him to place it on his head. In the end, after having thus given up everything, did the king feel any remorse or bitterness? No. In fact, this is what he said: "Thank you God for your grace. Indeed, when we become blind with pride due to our wealth, you, by taking away our money, give us back our eyes" (Srimad Bhagavatam 8.22.5). This was the glorious Bali who gave up his all to the Lord.

Jharokha (Window) Painted with King Bali Pledging Himself to Vamana Avatar of Vishnu

Conclusion:

These are the nine ways in which we can relate to God. We are free to select the particular connection with God which suits our personal temperament. However remember that all these nine qualities existed together in the Bhaktas mentioned above. Did Arjuna not have Pada Sevana, Smarana etc? Of course he did. For us this means that once we have imbibed even one of these virtues properly, all others will follow suit, and the person becomes a Shuddha Bhakta, one whose each and every action can be deemed as Bhakti.

Ashrams

Ashram means "a place of spiritual shelter." Each stage of life is not only a natural part of the journey from cradle to grave, but a time at which spirituality can be developed.

The four *varnas*, accept *ashrams* as depicted in the table below:

	BRAHMA CHARI	**GRIHA STHA**	**VANAPRA STHA**	**SANNYASI**
Shudra	No formal education	yes	no formal retirement	no formal sansnyasa
Vaishya	yes	yes	no formal retirement	no formal sannyasa
Kshatriya	yes	yes	yes	no formal sannyasa
Brahmin	yes	yes	yes	yes

Today, only a few Hindus strictly follow all these four *ashrams*. Nonetheless, the idea of enjoying the world in a religious and regulated manner, followed by gradual retirement remains a powerful ideal. Each of the four *ashrams* has its specific duties. The main ones are listed below.

Brahmachari (Student Life)

The *brahmachari-ashram*, often away from the home (somewhat like a boarding school), was primarily intended for fostering spiritual values. Memorisation and skill development were subsidiary to character formation and self-realization. Even sons of the royal family were expected to undergo this austere and rigorous training.

To be celibate and live a simple life, free from sense pleasure and material allurement.

To serve the guru (spiritual teacher) and collect alms for him.

To hear, study and assimilate the Vedas.

To develop all the appropriate qualities: humility, discipline, simplicity, purity of thought, cleanliness, soft-heartedness, and so on.

Grihasta (Household Life)

Traditionally some men remained lifelong celibates, either remaining as *brahmacharis* or immediately becoming *sannyasis*. Others were required to marry, extending their responsibilities to include wife, children, relatives, and society in general. This *ashram* is the only one permitting sexual gratification.

- To make money and to enjoy sensual pleasure according to ethical principles.
- To perform sacrifice and observe religious rituals.

- To protect and nourish family members (wife, children, and elders).

- To teach children spiritual values.

- To give in charity, and especially to feed holy people, the poor, and animals.

Vanaprastha (Retired Life)

After the children have left home and settled, a man may gradually retire from family responsibilities and, with his wife, begin to focus his mind on spiritual matters. Often he goes on pilgrimage. His wife may accompany him, but all sexual relationships are forbidden. *Vanaprashta* literally means "forest-dweller."

- To generally devote more time to spiritual matters.

- To engage in austerity and penance.

- To go on pilgrimage.

Sannyasa (Renounced Life)

This position is traditionally available only to men who exhibit the qualities of a *brahmana*. The man would leave home and family and was prohibited from seeing his wife again. Considered civilly dead, he was free to wander, living a life dependent on God alone. The *sannyasis* are conspicuous in their saffron dress. They are often called *sadhus* (holy people) – although today not all are genuine!

- To fully control the mind and senses, and to fix the mind on the Supreme.

- To become detached and fearless, fully dependent on God as the only protector.

- To teach and preach the importance of self-realization and God-consciousness, especially to the householders, who often become distracted from their spiritual duties.

Meaning and Purpose

- What does the system of four ashrams say about the purpose of life, according to Hindu thought?

Personal Reflection

- Do these stages resemble what happens in other societies? If so, what are the similarities? What are the differences?

- Are there any values which stand out for us, or with which we strongly agree or disagree? Why?

- How is our evaluation of these practices coloured by our own world view and our own culture and upbringing?

Conclusion

Who is God.Who is I.What is World. These are the serious questions that always arise in mind. Various communities in the World have various ideologies and following as per their climate,social and political Environment. Most have their own book of Ideology except Sanatan (Hinduism) community people following seriously. Mostly the community reciting the Ideology Book and people think this is the talk of GOD.

After deeply study of the GITA and other Ideology of different different Community our finding is as under-

1. Most people in the world accept the GURU and people accepting the talk of GURU is the talk of GOD.Hence quality of Guru is most important.People accept the Guru on three basis.

a. GURU who has Practical knowledge of Universe.Miracle happening and people accepting him GOD.GURU teaching and writing technical books to understand and follow the technology.

b. GURU who have power of Economy.Money is the matter of all facts,hence GURU is powerful in Economy becoming GOD for Human who is getting benefit from him and people following the ideology as prepared by him.

c. GURU who are capable of satisfying the dissatisfied multiple women or supporting the multiple women for peaceful living,GURU becoming popular and following their Ideology blindly.

2. Three qualities of human beings,Satva,Rajas and Tamas can be controlled by control of Sense,Mind,Intellect and Self Control.

3. Community surrendering to one Ideology Book after death of Ideology founder has become serious for the Community and Society,because Ideology is changing as per Climate,Country,Time Changing.

4. In the World all communities follow the Science of GITA,systematically following 16 Sanskar for valued Life and Ritual Purity includes Family Purity.

5. 16 Sanskar and Ritual Purity includes Family Purity is the technical and essential truth of life and it needs to be understood and followed systematically for a valuable Journey of LIFE.

6. Actions based upon Sacrifice(Yagya),Charity(Dan) and Penance(Tap) should never be abandoned,they must certainly be performed. Acts of Sacrifice,Charity and Penance are purifying even those who are wise. Why Action is required is as different view as under-

a. Devotion to the Creator, truthful living, and service to humanity is the will of every human.

b. Healing, Maintenance of Health and Protection is a requirement of each human being.

c. Good Thoughts,Good Words,Good Deeds.is the assets of LIFE.

7. Most people do not understand the definition of GOD.
Who is GOD?

a. Each Element in human beings is in the same ratio as in Nature,Every Creature is a particle of Nature.Such as Human is built withAkash(5%Sound),Air(6%Sense),Fire(5%Formation),Water(72 %Taste)andearth(12%Smell),Mind(alwaysinmovement),Intellect(k nowledge) and Ahankar(Ego).Nature is also built with following element in same ratio.

b.   Each Element is in similar proportion in childhood.This is changing after undisciplined activity which is against Nature.

c.   In Today condition, mostly city or Town is with poor air quality ,Water quality is poor,Food quality is poor, and even Environment of living is poor.In this condition when poor health people meeting with yogi who is seriously practicing yoga meditation and living in natural environment,people gets immediate benefit.In temple where pujari performing puja and creating a living environment.Once poor health people enters the temple people get energy and miracle happening to them.

d.   GOD is who energizes the poor health people.Poor health does not mean only ill health,but differences in VAT,PIT and KAPH and status of Greed,Attachment & Anger.

8.   The following technology is required to stay near to Nature such that-

a.   Work is the Prime requirement of Human beings,hence WORK IS WORSHIP.

b.   Nature is controlling every creature in Nature,hence every human has to work without any materialist attachment.Result is offered by Nature.

c.   Chanting of Mantra,Arti,Sloka,Goddess geet,music,or epic like Ramayna,dancing is good for health,it cleans the mind and controls anger,greed and attachment.

d.   Every Creature and human being needs to surrender to Nature itself . Inner Energy is needed for strength,Controlling the Sense,Mind and Intellect is essential to control activity, Self control is essential to understand Self and Nature and Peace Pranayam to reach Samadhi.

I. Anyone can Surrender to nature to perform Shiva/Surrender/Naman Pranayam.Sit down in Vajrasana watch the joined hand(Mother Energy living in Joined Hand).Take Deep breath (Inhale) and up the joined hand.Outhale the breadth and bring head to earth without removing Butt from leg.Take Deep breath and back to sitting position.Outhale and return to Vajrasana position.Continue for 21 to 108 times.

II. Performing of KUMBHAKA Pranayama controlling the Inner Energy.This is happening as first Inhale respiration,put outer kumbhak for few second further Outhale,put Inner kumbhaka and as on.Continue for 11-11 cycle each.

III. To control the Sense,Mind and Intellect-Equalise the Inhale and outhale to bring mind in Third Eye position.Contine for 21 cycles.

IV. To Control the Self, Perform self control Meditation.Watch the Inhaling and Outhaling to bring Mind at door of Nose,once mind is controlled means mind is staying to watch from 1 minute to 30 minute.Start to watch sensation outer part of body from top to Bottom without reaction in sensation.Once Free flow condition achieved,watch inner part of body and no reaction in any sensation,in inner also free flow condition will reach.It Controls the Human body leads to Immortal in Life.

V. Development of Mangal Maitri condition(Be like an Umbrella) is causing free from ill health.

- Continuous practice of Self Control Meditation is a good method to increase the Mangal Maitri.

- Regularly joining the 12 day Upnayan Sanskar Programme brings Mangal Maitri condition for 24x7x365.

- Volunteering Continuous Services in Temple or in Society is a good method to increase the Mangal Maitri.

- Continuous Chanting of Hare Rama Hare Krishna is also a good step to increase the Mangal Maitri.

- Control of the Anger,Greed and Attachment is also a way to increase the Mangal Maitri.

- Sacrifice and Service without attachment is the way to increase the Mangal Maitri.

- Sanyasi,Pujari,Sacrifice and service without attachment in Temple/Mosque/Church/Gurudwara is a way to increase the mangal Maitri

VI.   Those who will bring Permanent Peace in Life,has to practice the Peace Pranayam in which Bring Mind and Respiration to Anahat Chakra and stop the Anger,Greed and Attachment.Once stabilize,bring Mind and Respiration to Third Eye position with no anger,greed and attachment,once stabilize further bring Mind and Respiration to Crown Chara,once it reaches the Mind,Respiration and body will leave each other and people getting permanent Peace or Samadhi.

Further Study

AYURVEDA SCIENCE is the real requirement to study further to deeply understand the Science of Nature ,Science of Human Body and Science of Life.

Bibliography

The Internet is the media who gives all study material,photographs to read the Ideology of all communities and Gita from Gita Press is studied for this Research.

www.ingramcontent.com/pod-product-compliance
Lightning Source LLC
LaVergne TN
LVHW030007180726
843489LV00009B/3205